The Inevitable Threesome

Written & Illustrated by

Dyamund D

The Inevitable Threesome

Author: Dyamund D

ISBN: 978-1-83853-690-9

Publisher: Independent Publishing Network

www.dyamunddcreations.co.uk

info@dyamunddcreations.co.uk

wattpad DyamundD

@DyamundD

YouTube Dyamund D Creates

SOUNDCLOUD Dyamund_D_Creates

Copyright © 2021, Dyamund D

All rights reserved.

No part of this publication may be reproduced, stored in a retrieval system, stored in a database and / or published in any form or by any means, electronic, mechanical, photocopying, recording or otherwise, without the prior written permission of the publisher.

I dedicate this book to my Mum and Dad who came together in love during the bloom of youth, to produce a rare, one of a kind and complex individual. Separately they both gave me words that ping around my skull on a daily.

Dad - *"Don't let anyone ever tell you 'you don't know' because they don't know what you know!"*

Mum - *"Always know why you are doing something."*

CONTENTS

PREFACE

LIFE

Life Intro - 11

1. Life - 13
2. Current - 14
3. R.E.S.P.E.C.T - 15
4. What it is! - 16
5. Seduced by the Miami Sun - 19
6. Rain Drops - 21
7. Office Life (Or lack thereof) - 23
8. Communicate we shall - 28
9. People, Person, Human, Homo-sapien - 29
10. Uninterrupted Aqua - 31
11. Do your thing - 32
12. Life's Rhythm - 33
13. Contracts and Contacts - 37
14. Confused - 38
15. Shades of Darkness - 41
16. Art of Word - 42
17. Verano '18 - 45

LOSS

Loss Intro - 50

1. Loss - 51
2. Displaced - 52
3. Moment - 55
4. Breezy - 58
5. It's ALL on Me - 60
6. Repetition - 64
7. Value - 66
8. Connected - 69
9. Most of my time - 72
10. Control - 78
11. Muerte - 82
12. Letting go - 84
13. Au revoir - 86

LOVE

Love Intro - 88

1. (Ode to) Love - 90
2. A-Z of Love - 91
3. My Empress - 93
4. Conscientious - 95
5. Dayzenites - 96
6. Eye Yell - 98
7. King for a Queen - 100
8. Equilateral - 102
9. Beast - 104
10. Together. Forever. Never. - 107
11. Fun and games - 110
12. Twilight Cavorting - 112
13. Circlinity - 115
14. Adieu - 120

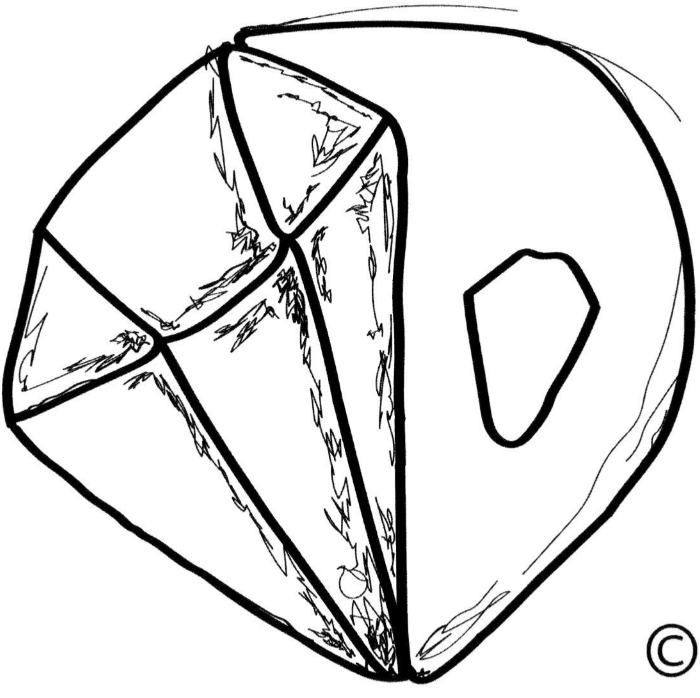

PREFACE

This book has been created as a means of allowing my creative passions to flow in a medium that I love - poetry and visual art. These feelings for the arts were laying dormant for many years as I walked a path that never felt natural or normal.

I am a creative born who has been living in a world of analytics, data and straight lines.

For a long time I felt I needed to step out and away from the confines of the work that I had decided to commit myself to and share my story in a way that could be both exciting and informative for those who care to indulge me.

These writings are a combination of my thoughts and feelings, written using various methods and styles that I hope you can learn from and share with others. If any message resounds with you or you feel will be useful for others to know then the desired effect has been reached.

There has always been an aspiration to write a book of poetry and in my heart it came to a point where there was *'no time like the present'* and so I got stuck in. My desire was to manifest a book that existed as an art piece in its entirety.

My labour of love.

Life

Here is a collection of poems about *'the self'* and my many observations of life. When I say 'the self' I am referring to your whole being; emotions, thought process, energy output and the external forces that shape the development of these.

Although relatively young, I have experienced a significantly varied life. This has enabled me to have an outlook on life that has not been restricted by my societal upbringing.

Sometimes it is hard to know or see where we fit in this world, especially as everything can be an influence. These poems are an insight into my perspective of life. I have included a collection of other perspectives that I've heard or observed over time and channeled my thoughts to allow them to be manifested into an artistic form.

Expressing how various experiences affect us can be difficult. With the beauty of language that we have, it is within our power to depict how we observe the world as clearly as our hearts desire.

There is not a single person on this planet that can tell you how you do, will or should see the world.

In my experience, I have accepted that life is a journey with no end. Whether I act or stand still, everything and everyone will continue and sometimes it is OK to pause and collect my thoughts. The moment we stop due to difficulties, hardships and the natural stumbling blocks that occur, we have effectively given up on life.

Something to remember is that *'everything is temporary'* whether good or bad. So ride the rollercoaster of life on the up and when it starts speeding downwards, hold your hands high and enjoy the trip. Things will start going the other way again... Eventually.

There is a beauty in being alive that can repeatedly be bypassed.

The many clichés that we hear around us can be true, if we take the time to *'stop and smell the roses.'*

The tranquility of a sunrise, the wonderful sound of a gentle breeze in the tree leaves at springtime.

Or the crying of a new born baby; breathing life into a new world and love into their parents.

Think about how delicious and refreshing a mouthful of water tastes on a hot summers day.

We do not always have to experience the elaborate and fanciful to appreciate the glory of life.

One thing you must ensure you do is be open to life's lessons.
In the positive or the negative, take *'the rough with the smooth.'*
That is one way you can maintain your mental strength.
To endure whatever comes at you (and you will - if not already – have experienced some unbelievably challenging circumstances) and be able to continue to strive for your desires with life's everlasting journey.

Time to stand.

Walk and travel your road of existence.

LIFE

A funny thing that situation, life!
Full of surprises, humour and strife.
Twists and turns are plentiful,
Worth living eventful.
Gotta give a shout out to the midwife.

Challenges overcome make us diamonds,
Nuff people front, we all get frightened.
Fear of the unknown, normal.
Intense feelings audible.
Pleasure seekers' senses are heightened.

Yesterday, today and tomorrow,
Jump between joy, surprise and sorrow.
We plan for the next story,
No guarantees of glory.
Friends you can count on, things you can borrow.

Guns 'n' knives breed blood and guts, heaps of war,
Soldiers fight to fix a Generals score.
Battlefields and casualties,
Postcodes and tragedies,
Streets meet warriors deadly to the corp.

Adventures span from estate to estates.
Travel by planes, trains, bikes and skates
Intrepid explorer.
No need to hold a corner.
Oysters for everyone and their mates.

Delights for the senses fill the belly,
Michelin star, fast, fine, ready for telly.
Roast or sautéed it's all good!
Some great spots in da hood!
Niceness; Jerk, Jollof or vermicelli.

A funny thing that situation, life!
Full of surprises, humour and strife.
Each persons story unique,
Memoirs shared, interests pique.
Cities booming, uncurbed loss of wildlife.

CURRENT

As I sat in the room I looked,
Left to right, left to right...not a clock in sight.

I wondered, I pondered and I conjured,
A plan on how to be the man,
The man I must become to make proud my mum.

Father, no longer will you poke and prod,
But rather give me that slow and acknowledgeable nod,
Of realization,

We are man.

Standing on the forefront of life imagining what is to come,
With a remembrance of the past when the future would never be.

Right now, right here,
We live in the present,
This is when we have all the fun,
Each passing moment a blessing to be shared with a loved one.

As I sat in the room I looked,
Left to right, left to right...not a clock in sight.
I wondered, I conjured a plan on how to be the man, the man I must become, the man I will be, and the man I am today.

Current.

R.E.S.P.E.C.T

*R*omantically engaged, sometimes people expect certain traits.

*E*ncouraging synchronisation promotes easier companionship & tactility.

*S*timulate, protect, engage calmly; treasure.

*P*assion evokes continued thoughtfulness.

*E*pitomising conscientious togetherness.

*C*ommunication throughout.

*T*rust.

WHAT IT IS!

Fiendishly barbaric,
Mercilessly savage,
Pitilessly cruel,
Ruthlessly brutal,
Outside world

Affectionately tender,
Competitively devoted,
Lovingly warm,
Thoughtfully caring,
Home life

Educationally instructed,
Academically learned,
Studiously attentive,
Perceptively astute,
School system

What it is, is what it is and it could never be what it wasn't.
But what it could be is what you want, if what you want is what it is.

Barbarism exists for the barbaric,
Mercy does not belong to the merciless,
Pity is not deserved for all,
Brutality makes you not a brute,
The world is as is, which is as it was

Reserve affections for the tender,
Respect competition, act with devotion,
Respond lovingly, embrace with warmth,
React thoughtfully, to understand caring,
Your home is yours, yours is for you

Eradicate educational errors,
Appreciate academic advantage,
Studiously suspend suppositions,
Promote powerful perceptions,
School teaches life, but life is school

What it is, is what it is and it could never be what it wasn't.
But what it could be is what you want, if what you want is what it is.

Fiendishly, schemers decide the fate of those unknowing,
Savagery ravages the streets, enveloping with a shroud of fear,
Cruelty appears to live at the fingertips of decision makers and rebels.
Ruthlessness sits at the heart of the fat cats eating lavishly,
The world is divided in two, haves and have not's, residing in category three

Affectionate people, embrace well, their love beautifully permeates your being.
Competitive souls bring a thrill and a chase, to elevate and progress
Lovely persons saunter past like a whisper on the ear, leaving tranquility alive,
Thoughtful folk, never take them for granted, upholder of peace and right,
Home is where the heart is; your heart is everywhere you go

Education teaches a great many, but still fools rush in - Love
Academia prepares for a life that doesn't read from a page – Live
Studious behaviour is not reserved just for the wise. Take heed - Listen
Perceive what surrounds, be astounded absorb the world, sponge like – Learn
School's out, life's in, prepare with the tools given, construct your world – Liberate

What it is, is what it is and it could never be what it wasn't.
But what it could be is what you want, if what you want is what it is.

SEDUCED BY THE MIAMI SUN

Seduced by the Miami sun,
Tenderly kissed on the forehead after a lingering glare

Embraced and caressed,
Longing for this moment to last forever

The burning heat and desire for one and other,
My skin crying out to be touched, licked from head to toe

Oooh our thirst so unquenchable
Clothes are ripped from my body, it's too intense
I need the warmth; I yearn to be immersed in the blinding beauty

Never before has the world witnessed a craving such as ours

Our time apart feels like an eternity...so cold...So Dark,
Hours turn to minutes and I see you,
almost glimmering on the horizon

Neither of us can wait, the world can set their watches by our rendezvous, our need to bask in the presence of one and other

This enchantment will live on into eternity,
Forever, together, always connected my Miami Sun
Seduced, my Miami Sun.

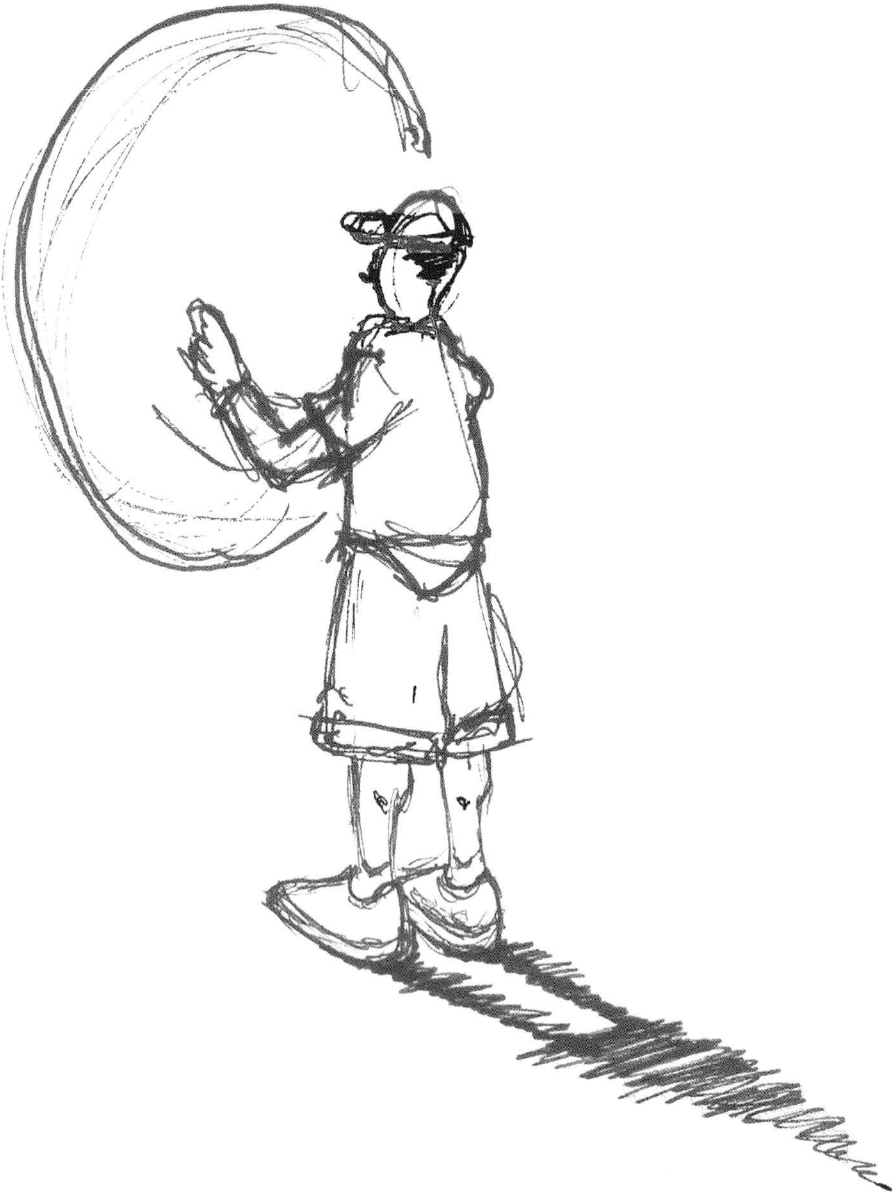

RAIN DROPS

Rain Drops descending, cleaning filth and grime.
Rapidly flowing, motion fluid as the hands of time.

Bringing moisture to earth's ground, clouds mightily subdue the sun.
Blamed for playtime wash outs, dampening of the fun.

Survival is hopeless without essential downpours.
A beach is not a beach without the seashore.

Bless your ears with the wet ambient sounds,
Listen carefully, let tranquillity resound.

Drops trickle effortlessly down the window, gathering in a pool.
Everywhere reflections and glimmering, these tiny precious jewels.

Thunder and lightning rages, but there was calm before the storm.
You just need to wait it out till the breaking of dawn.

The rain brings joy, to those stuck with a drought.
People desperately praying for precipitation to hastily come about.

Splash in a puddle, dance in the rain.
Such an exquisite experience, drying off, by a flame.

It keeps coming, gushing, encompassing, and flooding to envelope
all and everything: relentlessly.
Rain drops, the bringer of life and death. It has been there constantly
throughout man's history.

Love it,
hate it,
the rain has a job to do.

Without the H2O there'd be no me and there'd be no you.

OFFICE LIFE (OR LACK THEREOF)

As I sit here, looking around the cold interior of the grey matt walls, I wonder 'where did I go wrong?'

Saying I went wrong could be incorrect, because, who is to define what is right?
Living in a world where fear is the masses controller, have I succumb to the pressures of society?

Was this the future planned out for me? Destiny! A concept and a theory?

The friendships are loosely based on the commonality of the office politics; will they last beyond the contract?

Is that tick tick ticking and tap tap tapping the sound of me working my fingers to the bloody bone on the keyboard of misery and contempt?

Or is it Captain Chronos playing his chimes of time?

Will I last until another lunchtime or is my slow perishing body going to be consumed and emaciated by this hollow existence of office life?

Where should I be? Am I not the man of my own making, doing and creating?

My shadow is mine, my hair, nails and teeth belong to me, but my mind... is it mine?
Maybe I have to mine into my mind to know what is mine?

Reactions of external forces, forces me to make decisions that I could never foretell, but why?

Why? Why oh why? So many questions from management colleagues and comrades.

Whirling of machines, vomiting paper and defecating coffee all day bombard my ears.
Am I the one making them sick, sick of the overload for my mental and physical consumption?

I sit, I spin, I push, I twist, but am I anywhere different to the last 5? Alive?

It's a weird concept that fights to vanish from my mere mortal mind.
Am I furniture?

I watch as conversations unfold, the humans rebel against their dehumanisation.
Can I join the resistance?

Resistance is futile, your department, my department – loggerheads.
Is absconding possible?

The post I've been assigned to man, does not promote the man,
man oh man, am I man or mouse?

This mouse between my fingers doesn't wriggle and squirm,
no signs of life as though in my house. Can I leave?

Father time does a jig around my wrist, almost in sync with my heartbeat, is this corpse reanimating?

4:45pm Brain dead. 4:50pm electricity pulses, igniting life.
Chitter chatter, nitter natter it's 4:58. Is it that time?

Itchy feet, sweaty pits, all signs of life. This grey catacomb has had its fill of vampiric blood sucking. Can you draw blood from stone?

No. But can Stone acquire blood from you?

The hands of time scream 'five fifteen.'
One more injection of vitality, now's the time to make my escape?

Can I save my mortality?

The path is clear, the armed guards, with their seniority blockades have turned their backs. It's now or never!

"Oh, before you go, can you just…?"

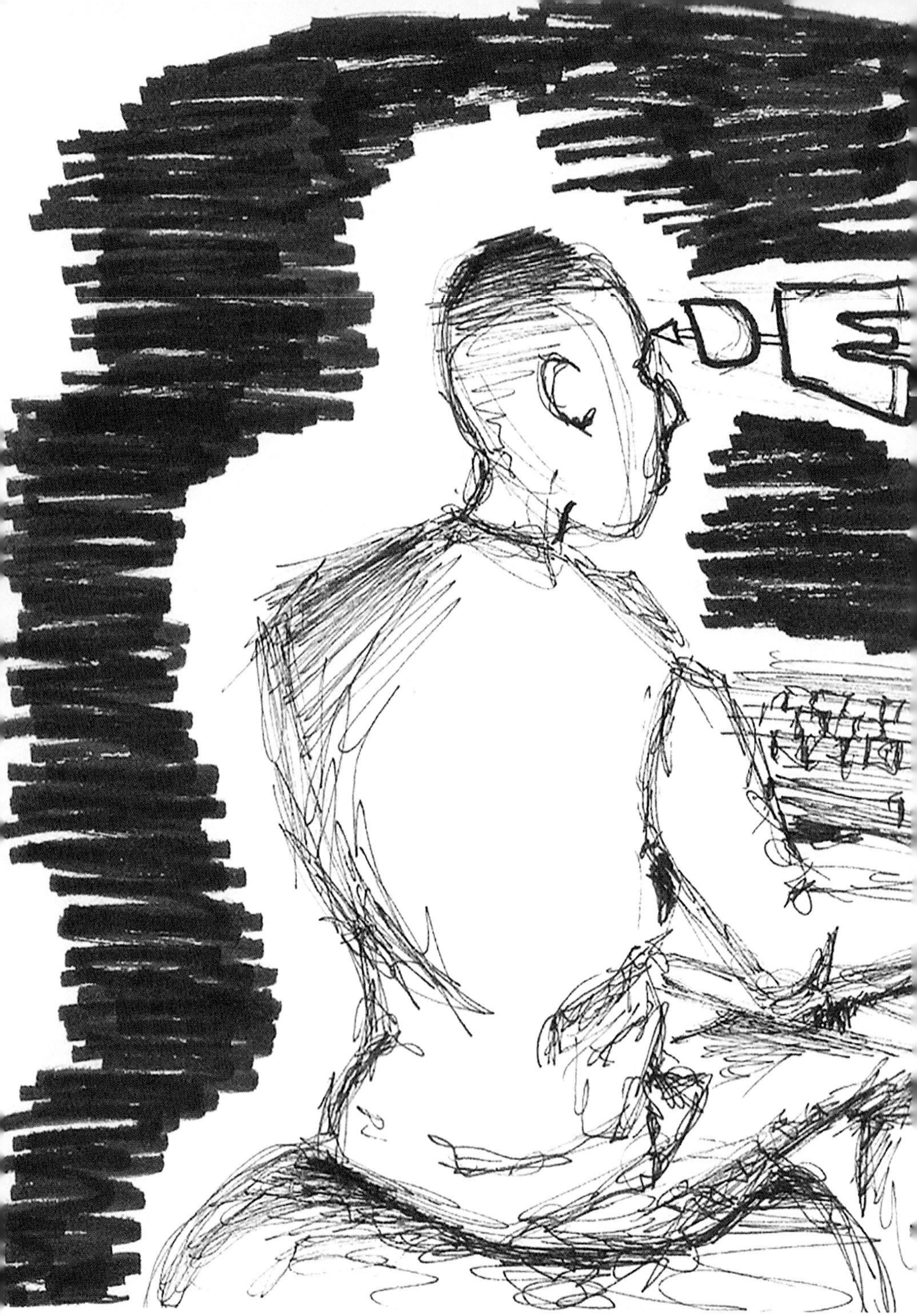

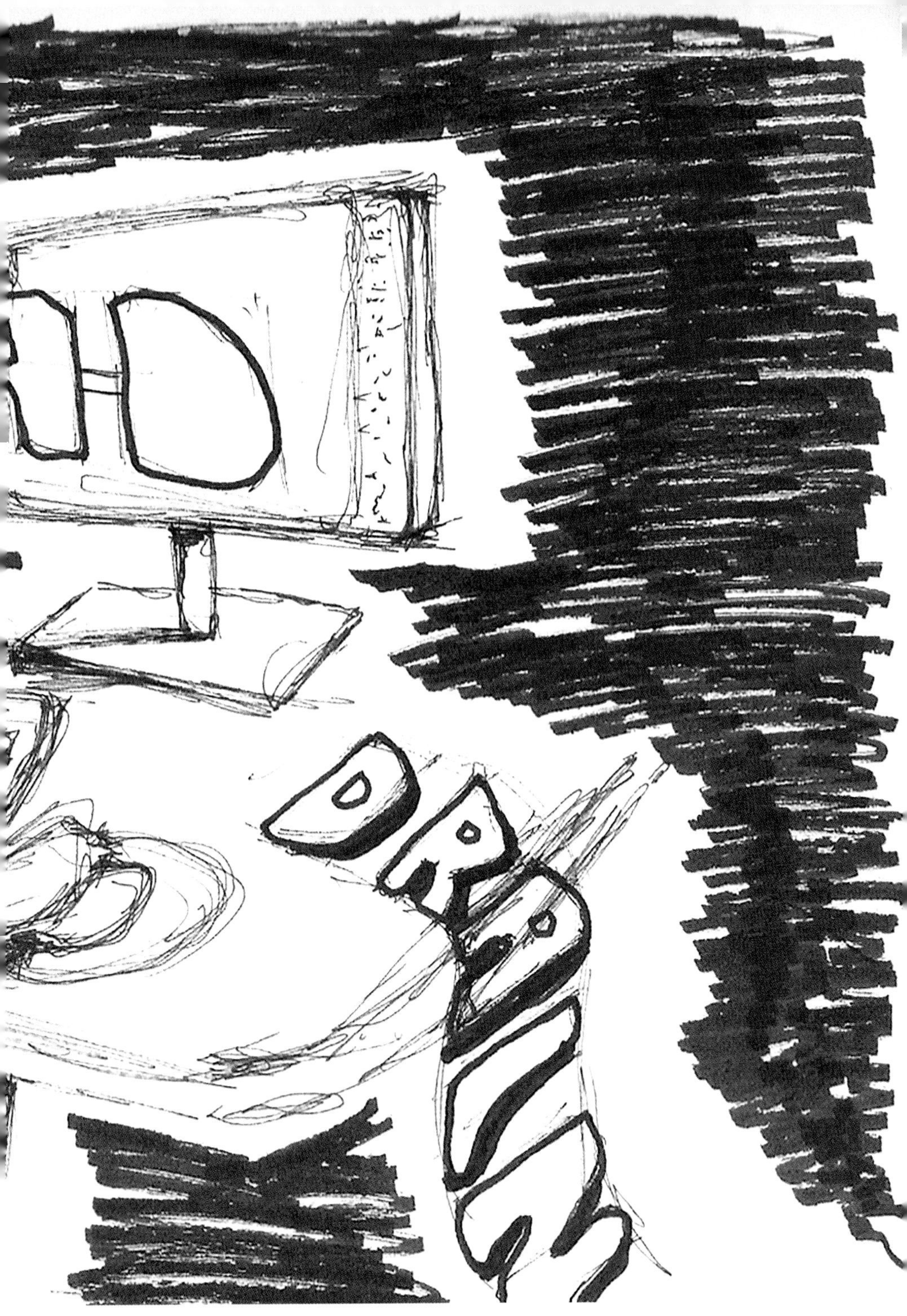

COMMUNICATE WE SHALL

It goes a long way to bring your P's and Q's to the party.
You've nothing to lose when being polite.
Manners make all the difference to your interactions.
Sometimes that 'thank you' can change a person's day.

Positive responses from strangers can be rather hearty.
Better to be warmly welcomed, than having to fight.
Never underestimate how this affects the power of attraction.
Meet and greet positively, get more invites to play.

That gesture oh so rude and offensive, that's so uncalled for
It has to be questioned if it's you or them.
Pride can bring the worst, even when hearts intend goodness.
Lofty and haughty are sure to bring ruination to attachments.

Struggles to placate the masses, daily, leaving the mind sore,
Impossible pleasing all, all the time, but try to mix and blend,
Difficult as it seems, lead each thought with pureness.
Positivity attracts like. Throw it out, extend your catchment.

Manners make all the difference,
Teach through action; kill ignorance.
Politeness comes at no mortal cost,
Centre yourself. Help others who are lost!

PEOPLE, PERSON, HUMAN, HOMO-SAPIEN

People are a strange enigma.

Full of twists and turns in every action and word.
Birth breeds openness and a boundless tongue,
Whilst growth promotes dishonesty and diplomacy.

Our relatives cannot be chosen, but family is carefully selected,
Friends come and go seasonally, but reside ever present, Mountainous.
We strive to understand one and other, often leaving bewildered.

Atrocities and acts of unbridled love live side by side,
With war waging, a love story will bloom; resembling springtime rose.
A seed planted blossoms into representative miniatures.

One Person can influence the many

Consumption of all that's witnessed without sight of satisfaction,
Mini revolts against the status quo, but challenging dictators is minimal.
Parties and jubilation aren't mutually exclusive, yet celebrations bind.

Once a man, twice a child! Signs of the old days.
Modern Man-child syndrome is rife.
Populations living longer, whilst the gaps between generations blur.

Homes of love and homes of fortune exist parallel,
Mans best friend conserves sanity and generates purpose.
Humans declare love for animals of wild, but destruction loves more.

Technology is defining our Humanity

Tribes of identical faces and different colours clash,
Languages automatically dominate and subjugate,
Whilst shared trauma collaborates the unsuspecting neighbours.

Charity begins at home, pilgrimage to the third abundant.
True support is found wanting, as talk is cheap.
Conferences placate the masses, when actions speak louder.

Humanities affection resides at the core of its being,
Translated through written word and shanty,
Education of each generation tells the tale.

Love conquers all as Homo-sapien flourishes

UNINTERRUPTED AQUA

It flows as though there is no end
Its origins charging the source
As the river runs
It seems not to wash away a thing

The stale and stagnant remnants of history are consigned to remain past
Nothing brought forward as time transpires
Memory drifts further back

Pathways to the great beyond travel southerly
Around the mouth gravity creates a flow of plummeting water

A drip
        A drop
                A splash and crash

Onlookers gaze at the familiar sight
Seen across the globe
Its story is different each and every time

DO YOUR THING

There was a man who loved to wear hats.
Not an animal fan, but he loved cats.
Every day he looked sharp,
A musician who played harp;
Super cool he had to show off his tatts.

                                        Performing for the famous and rich.
                                  The only time he was rid of his twitch.
                                            Tell friends stories a plenty
                                                So young, a man of twenty,
                                      He could even sing at high pitch.

Grateful he was for living the dream.
Best of the best, people called him the cream.
Humble yet confident vibe
Mingled with talented tribes.
As a musician he aimed for supreme.

                                      Not inspired by money nor fashion,
                                      Solely driven by musical passion,
                                            He chased what he loved.
                                            Attacked life from above,
                           Provoked world change with compassion.

LIFE'S RHYTHM

We rise, we fall, we shout, we call.
Life ebbs and flows, new births, families glow as they grow,
Make up and break up, but forever blood flows...
Thicker than water,
Blood doesn't secure love.

Built and held through trust, some know not the difference
between lust and love.
To leave the nest is a must; children require a shove,
With support from above, not below,
So that parental connection prominently shows,
Whilst they chase desires.

Death consumes, life resumes.

We move forward.

Visit a graveside, talk over ashes, funerals breed contention and
flashes, of days gone by, drawing tears from eyes.

Happy or sad, perfect reasons to cry all season.
Never leave them, in their time of need, 10 good deeds forever live
in the heart, but can be torn apart by a single seed of distrust,
which must be undone by a multitude of great works.
These works can hurt and be a burden if the heart is not behind it.

Straightforward life never is,
Strife forever gives, challenges.
Balance is,
Key to survive when living life on a knife-edge.
A pledge to danger for some equals fun,

maybe some theft.

Seeing another rising sun isn't by chance as you dance with death.
You learn your trade, whatever that is, giving yourself and time,
whether to secure wealth through work or crime. Lime on a beach,
building an empire from your seat.

Options - you can teach the beat of music and the arts to a hoard of students without being prudent,
Let it flow from the heart.
Share knowledge with those who forage for information,
Be a station,
A beacon of thought,
We all had to be taught a thing or two; this time the master is you.

Do what you do as you do it best; never rest as life's a constant test.
Success or failure is in your hands; will you stand or fall when your backs against the wall and things get tough?

Enough is enough!

Only the strong will survive and heed the call of destiny.
Some crumble to the knee and pray for better days.

We work, we play, we aim to enjoy each day, most of us on a hunt
for that life partner,
that soul mate,
that play mate,
that... consistent date.
Don't hesitate when you see the one or it can be done in the blink
of an eye.
Never shy, press on and grab that companion with zest.
Relationships are not formed for free; build that bond, driven by
the pounding muscle in your chest.

We all need a hustle to achieve the greatest results.
A bolt of energy, a light bulb idea to hold real tight,
that's what many dream of,
running on steam,
push to the end, which is never in sight.

All your efforts go unnoticed unless making a big bang, no time for faking
or hanging around.
Pound for pound you are the best you in town.

Make money, have some laughs, procreate and it all starts again.
Life's rhythm, sweet as honey.

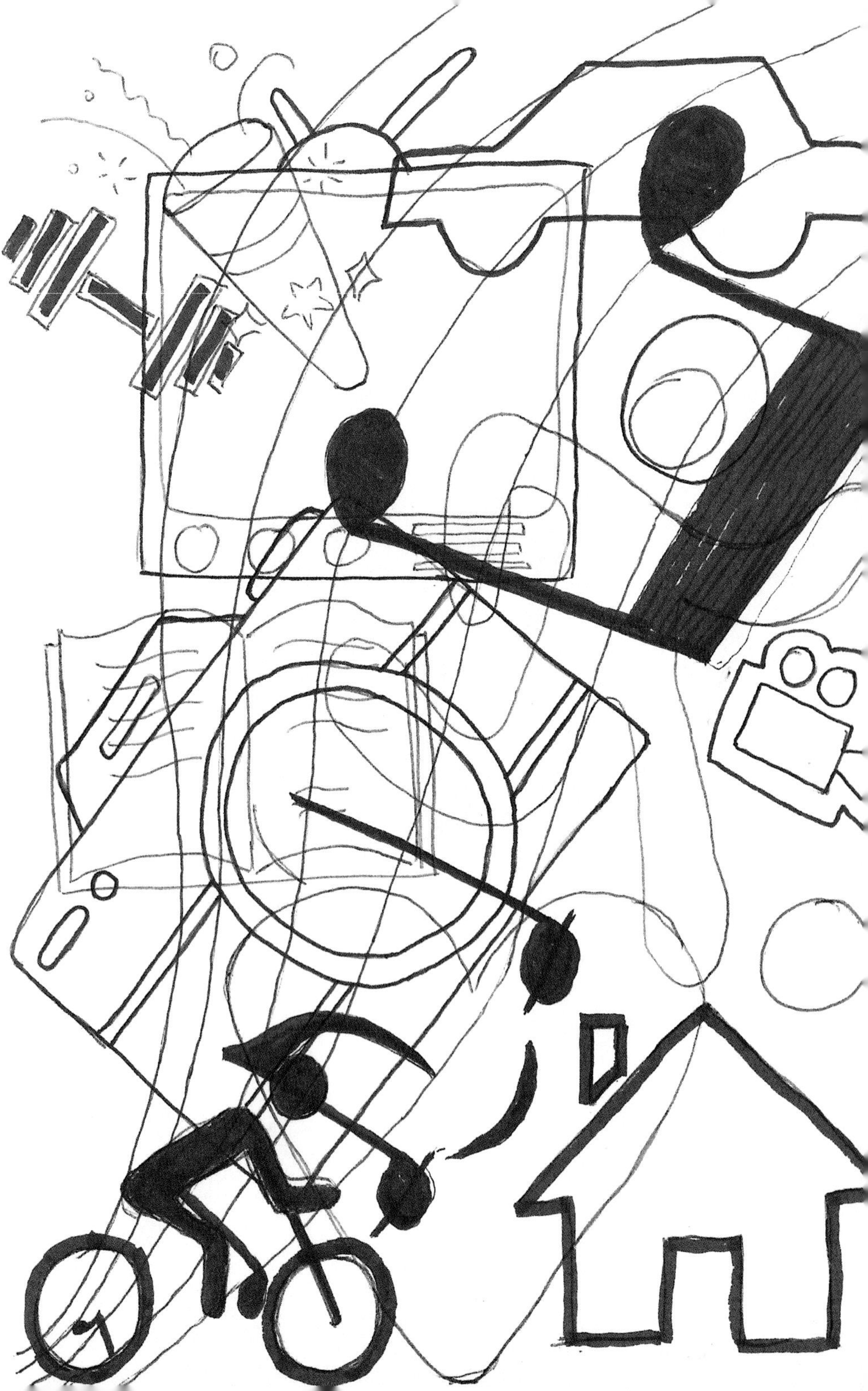

CONTRACTS AND CONTACTS

Faces frantically figuring out facts.
Forgetting feelings.
Frugal, finances find fault in errors of humanity.
Hands helplessly holding handles with hot contents, hoping home hypostatizes swiftly.

Computers continuously call countless codes and calculations for work,
people produce problems and plight with a necessity of precision,
solutions paramount.

Hierarchy holds us hostage. Hoping hours humour heads, resulting in financial hoisting.
Lunch leaves belly full, minds wondering. Lusting longingly for leniency of lacklustre labour.

Absconding annually allows for revitalisation,
returning ready to attack assignments aggressively.
Minds manifest motives, teams combine to move mountains miraculously,
goals gigantic broken down, accomplished greatly by grounds given.
Work whets life's worth with a desire to widen wisdom and win with appreciation,
contracts cease consequently.

CONFUSED

I am confused, I know I should do right, but I want to do left.

So many thoughts swirling around, yet a decision needs to be made.
There's a ringing in my ears or is it the misunderstood voice of my conscience?

Will I live for pain or pleasure? I may just do both.

Definitely, major heart stealer, that's what I should be, grand theft.
More fun being the bad guy, live a life of danger, lurk in the shade.
Money needs making, get a job and work hard... Na that's nonsense.
Play the elusive card, you want me, meh, not sure I want you.
Ghost!

That old cliché, something so wrong shouldn't feel so right.
Dipping a toe in, just to test out the waters or should I just dive headfirst?
Sitting on the fence you get the perfect view,
the grass is definitely greener.
I am tantalised, the prospects are immense, should I make moves?

Nothing there to stop me, I am a man of my word, get out my sight.
Naughty or nice, I can change like the wind; the only consistency is my thirst.
I love to joke as a serious guy, always upfront hiding like a champion schemer.
Shoulda, woulda, coulda, question me, you'll get no answer! I've nothing to prove.

This confusion could lead me to a path of excellence or a dicey road of death.

Either way time rolls on, ticks away
regardless of who I be.
At some point choice may be taken out of my hands,
am I prepared?
Youth is on my side but some day I will be
ravaged by time, an old man.

Surely none of this matters, as long as whatever
I do takes away my breath.
Chronological clashes, I'm not sure who will win,
but I need to construct
my history.

These thoughts, these feelings, I have opened up.
It has to be shared.
Accept me in all my shining glory, flaws and virtues
because I am who I am.

Mirror man you confused soul.

40

SHADES OF DARKNESS

You call me **Black**, but that means nothing to me, as that is neither
a language spoken or destination I know.
You call me **Black**, the darkest of colours representing much that is negative,
stripping all identity.
You call me **BLACK**! An intricate, yet simple method of portraying
the polar opposite image to all that is right, like snow.
You call me **BLACK**! This elicits no feeling, instigating
dehumanization, negating my true and vibrant history.

You call me **BlacK**, there's no way of me overstanding who I really am,
if this is the categorisation I choose to adopt.
You call me **BLack**, as this is the way you desire the world to view me.
A darkness, a mark and a blemish on society.
You call me **Black**. So does everyone else. There is no respect attached,
I can see it in your eyes and mannerisms. Stop!
You call me **Black**. Purveyors of racism as a Black man, Black
woman and **Black** child, live by limited description. Notoriety.

You call me **black**, I have a family, we laugh, play, sing, joke, argue and love.
Just like any other, we have affluence.
You call me **black**, our music harmonises our lives,
a gentle reminder of the tropical lands you love to holiday.
You call me **black**; admire our art, architecture, fashion, style and innovation.
Our cultures have influence.
You call me **black**, appreciate our differences; our diversity brings a
plethora of treats to the table, no dismay.

Take the black back; give me more, as before you once called me
moor as guests upon these shores.

ART OF WORD

Intricacies of the woven word entwine the mind and the world we exist in.
Twisting and turning, contorting into symbolism and imagery.
Unbelievably entrapped between soliloquies and dialogues of nonsense and intelligence.
Do you know me? Hello, how are you? Good-bye my friend, simplicity of language.
Quantum, actuarial, anthropometrics: Science so simple. Befuddle the many.

Salut, comment allez vous? Hola, como estas?
Language leaps and bounds across rivers, trees, land and floats across the air.
Entangled in a net, words struggle to be free from, the mind desiring to be comprehended,
Just as a web of lies is untangled, to be understood by sufferers of the consequences.

What? Why? Where? When? Who? How?
Construct, close, open and destroy forced together letters and marks on a page.
Weave and interlock like lovers lips, words saunter ear bound, a whisper of sweet nothings.
Monologue of the idiot can be made sense if those heeding the message overstand,
We understand as we understood those standing over us with power and instruction,
But overstand what needs to be overstood to relinquish influence of oppression.

History is his story but he is who? The story is what story and why is he telling it?
My story is mine to be known by those who know and knew what I spoke,
Speak of the ins and outs of the lives I've writhed, wretched, strung and slid through.
Punctuation puts points, answers, demands, facts and fiction to the test.

Slithering effortlessly off the tip of the tongue, but the tip of the iceberg is all that surfaces. As all is revealed the unknown becomes known as we don't know what we don't know. Words creeping incredulously towards one and other, as the owners know not of what they say. We decipher between true and false, painting pictures of the world without colour or shape. Clarity is sweeping the minds over time, exposing purposes and direction of the day.

Conjoined twins make sounds almost inaudibly different to individuals, but visuals differentiate. Silence is golden, but often confuse the young as they learn to form their own version of life. To learn is to lean on one and other, mimicking what is seen with a requirement to concentrate. Absorbing the right thing at the right time, for the perfect place, space and audience. Sublime is the picture presented, razor sharp, knife through butter, uneasy public expression.

Adulthood gives insight, but in sight is a mystery with he, her and it. Deviations unbound. Expectations of affectations without affections, but inspection of conversation exist. Then we see them, there by the sea, with their hair, blowing in the air, they should hear we are here. Learning that yearning brings burning sensations concerning earnings above animations.

VERANO '18

The heat was slow burning; embers of spring cooked away.
Sweat crept downward, creating a trail to the tools of love,
Smiles ripped faces in twain; mouths struggled to close.
People lay strewn across the horizon, BBQ sausages they became,
The sizzle of flesh was almost indistinguishable.

A dog's bark reverberated through every crevice of outdoors,
Skinny jeans replaced by batty riders, the men were fashionable;
White T's illuminated the roads, blinding eyes far and wide.
Food karts and vendors lazed in the heat, customers flocked,
Women became hot bread, doughy bodies appetizing.

Festivals were bountiful; the pleasure of attending evaded me.
The spirit of love and laughs lived brightly as a ball of hydrogen.
School uniforms became burdensome - 16 to 25 tantamount,
Mutton dressed up as lamb, well seasoned... An acquired taste.
Shirted, jeans fresh, crepes tasty, I feel like the sex!

Socials bring the respectable, debauched and luscious. Experiences are flavourful.
Rivers of 37.5 flow rapidly and freely, converging with seas of Spumante.
Worlds spin, eyes are blinded with rose and ships begin to sink,
Black mirrors glimmer in darkness, blue hue brightens the darkest corners.
Unknowns collaborate, strangers acquaint, future destinies written.

Absence of the starry light leaves a steamy atmosphere; it's sticky!
Rubber seduces stone, creating music with dancing fireflies, red and white.
Merriment cuts through the quietness of the trees whisper,
The sound of pre-pubescent youth is confined between bricks,
Escapism of the kiln is paramount, as bodies become water features.

One to be reckoned with, Junius battled Quintilis everything lead to Sextilis.
Stars aligned, summer dresses and bra's skirmished furiously.
Holidays wrestled credit cards and student loans till their final breath,
Immature relationships sang with temptation, offering multiple encores,
Vices were fought by the righteous. Battles lost but the war raged!

'Fun' names the season of hot flushes, cool drinks and warm nights,
Rampant delights, lads holidays and getaway flights.
Women be beautiful, their glory brightening each day.
A time that's naturally fruitful, I wouldn't have it any other way.

My Summer '18!

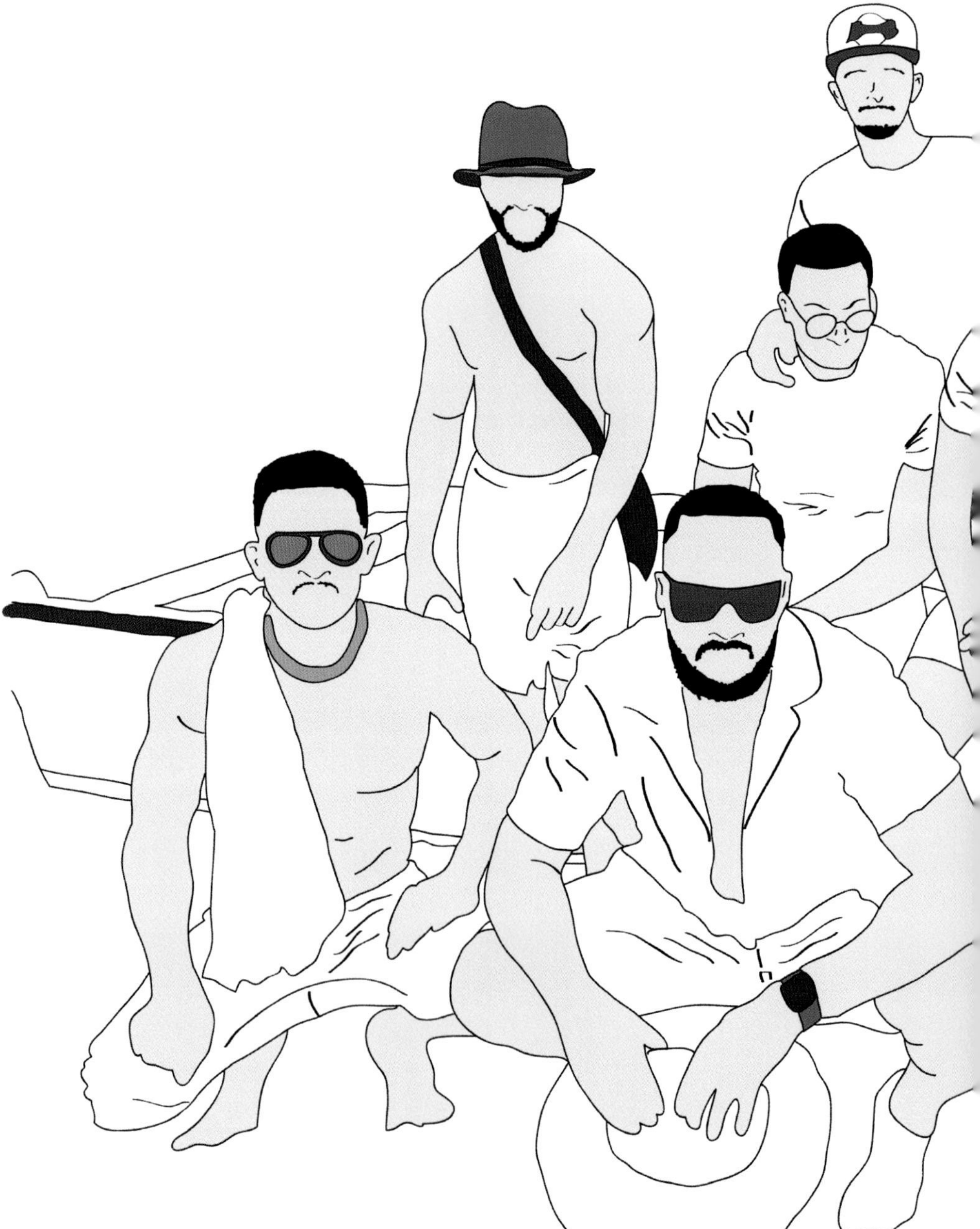

Loss

These poems depict the various loses we have in life; some of them are obvious and some not so much. We often go through life holding on to things that we shouldn't and often we can allow the true treasures to slip through our fingers.

Ofttimes we are unaware that we have lost something and the impact it has or may have on the rest of our lives. Without knowing, it is hard to counteract potential negative effects.

Many of the losses we have cause pain.

However there are instances where we require loss for personal development and to make the desired progress we want in life.

There is almost a perfect equilibrium between loss and gain. We must be well in tune with ourselves and the balance of the world to recognise it.

Due to the overwhelming negativity that we are bombarded with and is portrayed through a variety of mediums in our daily lives, we can easily lose sight of the positive. We lose time to gain money, education and experience in life.

The worse thing we can absolutely lose is our true selves.

Consumed by everything and everyone, 'me' can be absorbed into the void.

Resurfacing triumphantly is a battle that must not be lost.

We will be constantly tested and will need to maximise our resilience through discovery of self. Losses come with everything we do, in some form or other. nevertheless take the time to see what you have gained in return.

Appreciate the fact you are 100% unique, no carbon copies.
Reaffirm your authority to stand tall and be counted.

Lose the box and live boundless.

LOSS

Something we all have to face, is loss
Not a damn thing can be done
How we take it separates strong from weak
The transition period from past till now

Time can be stolen but never bought
But always comes at a cost
How the mature pine for their youth
Loss of our most valued commodity

Suffering usually denotes loss
This negative shroud delivers no fun
Nothing anyone desires to speak
Dig deep for triumph, be a plough

Only winning is ever sought
Life's no playground, harsh like winter frost
People afraid to lose face with truth
Pain of innocence lost, no oddity

Hard to face reality when losing
However temporary the strife
Childhood to adulthood the biggest debt
An unavoidable and crucial trial

We exchange time for money, begrudgingly
Surrender investments to acquire more
Catastrophe versus fortune is risk
Success awaits, while failure hangs above

Battle the bulge, lifestyle of your choosing
Junk is disposed for a healthier life
To lose the belly, encourage a sweat
Escape your comfort zone; reveal a smile

Spouses self sacrifice lovingly
Interdependence costs freedoms when sure
Put it all on the line, take a risk
You can lose your mind while falling in love

DISPLACED

Take me home. Right back to the place I've never been.
Wild animals, guerrillas and starvation are the only things I've ever seen.

The narrative is one that depicts a life I'll never love.
Some things must be experienced to know if it's ever enough.

Lion kings and black panthers reside in a place full of pride.
A mother's land is there to flourish; bloom. Abundant in life, ready to provide.

Musical melodies lead by dramatic drumbeats, bodies full of rhythmic jolts.
Colours speak of blood and a fight for freedom, passion full of revolt.

Languages with extraordinary variety depict a world of vastness.
Tribal scars and battle wounds, tell tales of lives in a world of harshness.

Nubian skin glistens beneath the sun and refracts the moon, oh so powerful.
A clear depiction of the origins of your origins, oppression oh so sorrowful.

White teeth against an ebony backdrop, paints a magically joyful picture.
Media tells of only flies on eyes, skin and bones, a tragically truthful picture.

Skyscrapers, mansions and highways. Diamonds and gold, story of the rich.
Mud huts, gravel road and red sand, tale of the poor, the story has been switched.

Lies upon lies, layers of deceit. No encouragement to journey back home.
Truth be told, many a time it's been said 'You should go back home!'

Rebels and coups, no peace shall ever exist. Danger lurks, unsafe from dawning,
Warm and welcoming, diaspora brothers and sisters. Family we are from morning.

There's no better place than England, streets paved with gold, those are facts!
Sun, fresh food, music and vibrancy, on second thoughts, bags are packed!

54

MOMENT

We always have time. Wasting it is no crime... foolishness.

One moment!

Just a moment!

I'll be there in a moment!

Just give me a moment!

Hold on for one moment!

Everything can change in a single moment.

Lives are lost in the blink of an eye - total chaos in that moment.
Things go from smiles to laughs, in one moment.
That young boy going to college: dead in that very moment.
Crime committed, thrill of the chase, games! In the docks, the judge changed their lives in that moment.

Carefree teenagers find out they're pregnant. Remembering it was all fun for that moment.

Things could have been totally different, if you paused for just one moment.

Those good times, those great times, those unforgettable times seem to last for a single moment.

Gaze upon your loved ones, cherish those precious moments.
A glance across the room at her and he knew she was the one,
in that moment.

The decision to change your life, takes just a single moment.
Create enjoyable experiences; we're here on earth just a moment.
Life is a one-way journey.
Don't waste your time on the insignificant, make the most of each and every moment.

Stop! Think!

Let the poem sink in for a moment.

BREEZY

Where has my youth gone?
Drifted away as the breeze blows upon the sea
Days were endless. Remember those summer songs?
Wrecking the school trainers, feeling carefree

What happened to those everlasting summer days?
Chasing man down, knock down ginger and a water fight
How comes no one said they'd go away?
Felt like an eternity, chilling, maxing and relaxing till night

How did things change so quickly?
Worrying about my new school bag,
Why could I never find my textbooks weekly?
Detention certainly on the cards, more jokes to be had.

Why has time zoomed past as though unencumbered?
First day in big boy school, exciting times!
Where's the warning signs my days were numbered?
Final exams, school done, no more school dinners. Waiting in line

How comes my clothes still fit saggy?
Looking like a '90s throwback, dem times dere, wicked!
What was I thinking with the extra baggies?
Still felt super slick, air max and a crisp shirt, vivid

When did I carve out this social spot?
Contemplating college, long! Everything ultra fresh,
How exciting, summer holiday and no homework plot?
New pastures, reinvention and more learning in the flesh

How am I years older, feeling and looking the same?
Friends are big and bearded a reflection of chronology
Where's my physical transformation to stop me being lame?
Minor, I'll still flex on them same way, garms look rough and gaudy

Where had my youth gone?
Floated away as a message bottle bobs upon the sea…
Days were timeless, who questioned if I'd grow up strong?
Wrecking trainers no more, missing life carefree,

IT'S ALL ON ME!

I am the victim and perpetrator of my own sins.
Through my eyes I see the gift and I see the curse that is me.
Thoughts and actions coincide to transport me to a place of my socalled choosing.

I inhale the positive and exhale the negative. What is to become of my soul?
Split straight down the middle I am a conundrum and a riddle, yet
straightforward and blank as a sheet of paper.

What I do has an impact on everything; with every action there is a, reaction.
Am I ready for the come back as the life pendulum swings?
Often, works divert from the desired outcome; complaints are not warranted.

To achieve is to believe in oneself, invest in self worth, health is true wealth.
The pursuit of more can leave you with less, if a severe lack of
appreciation is abundant, blessings lost: welcome stress!

I question, should I strive for greatness or live a life of satisfaction.
Many of those in power walk all over those who do not have.
Forgive and forget is asking a lot; but harbouring hate only hurts the one hating.

Each one, teach one, but is my consciousness available for learning?
"The mind is a terrible thing to waste," a desire for knowledge and growth,
I should be yearning.

Do as I say, not as I do. The mantra heard and witnessed of those who
have walked the earth before.
Walking my own seemingly unbeaten path can be painful and sore.

Look after the pennies and the pounds will look after themselves,
yet money is the root of all evil?
Striving for financial freedom can run you into cognitive imprisonment.

Telling myself needs must, but whom do I trust when it's time to do what needs to be done?
My wants can feel like needs, however progression dictates I need to want.
Do or die, but I'm not always dying to do, the results will speak for themselves.

Tomorrow is another day, but they say tomorrow isn't promised.
Plan for the future, but the best-laid plans often go awry.
Live for today as you only live once. Laziness may make me squander the now... perhaps till death I'll graft.

Living in the beginning, middle and end of my journey. I'm told as one door closes another opens.
So everyday I wake is another blessing, providing a chance to make my tomorrow better than today.

When all's said and done, I am the victim and perpetrator of my own sins.
Everyday I must walk the walk and talk the talk, to let time tell the tale that needs to be told.

It's all on me!

REPETITION

When you lose, it feels like a loss.
It's only a loss if you lose the lesson.
Lessons encourage advancement,
With each lesson tis win or lose.
It's not the taking part that counts.
You can lose if you choose, better to refuse!

Life's one long lesson, heed what's taught,
Make losing a learning curve.
Winners never quit and quitters never win.
Whether you win or lose, game continues,
Continuing to win is a formidable task.
You can lose if you choose, better to refuse!

Victory or defeat, a game of chess every interaction,
To be victorious is to know defeat.
Avoiding defeat is a mind-set of failure,
Planning victory sets up the success.
To be the best, you must beat the best.
Let victory not remain a mystery or reserved strictly for history!

To the victor the spoils, be in it to win it.
Be graceful when blessed with victory,
The higher you climb, harder the fall.
However attained, respect allegiances for victory is fleeting.
Where there is unity there is victory.
Let victory not remain a mystery or reserved strictly for history!

Success - the desire of man, woman and child,
Endeavour for power repeatedly achieved, but mustn't corrupt.
With great power comes great responsibility.
Only you can judge your successes,
Be sure to measure against your own ambitions.
Success has no excess, never repress your progress!

Media lead success portrays unrealistic expectations,
The success of others reflects on you not at all.
Money, power, respect, differentiators of success,
Family, friends and love, empowers the weak.
Success begets power to make life what you want.
Success has no excess, never repress your progress!

VALUE

How much is your life worth?
Prowling streets, unaware soon to be earth,
Shortening your existence like a school tie.
Blood bonds screaming goodbye,
Precious gifts disrespected.
Weight of the world brings the unexpected.

Youth does cloud all senses mystically.
All that glitters isn't gold, dreams sold,
Future decisions vanish, communal connectivity cut fatally.
Brain waves cease, police!
Tears bring rivers.
Sorrow drowns, fear what tomorrow delivers. Peace!

Value of breath priced. Gold chain.
Perception intimidates, down payment of severe pain.
Endings scarily unknown. Live like a king.
Religious ties, everybody sings,
Mournful days prolong.
Unforgettable smiles flitter away sharply. So long.

Essence wasted, absorbed into eternal nothingness.
Damned if you do. Think, just don't!
Smart moves confuse, befuddle enemies of progress,
Promote growth conscientiously, regularly.
Love brings life!
Unify brethren, await tomorrow, together in… Peace!

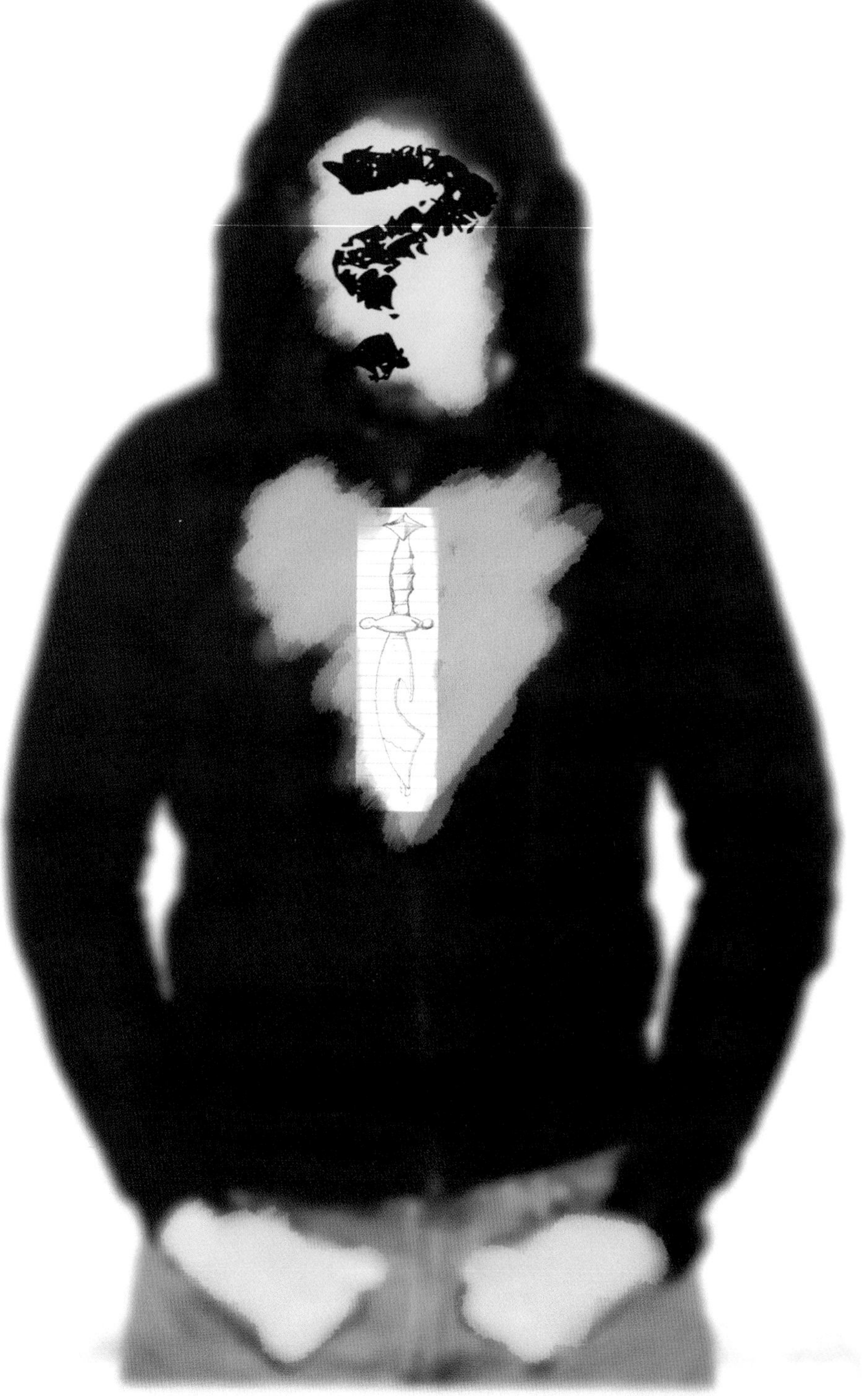

CONNECTED

When your mind wanders, your body doesn't follow.
Hollow, a machine with no pilot or purpose; yet, movement equals existence.
Inter-action, matters of faction. A belonging that isn't met!

Prove with cement, substance beyond the void - Grey matter and nitrogen base.
Paranoid delusions throw discombobulation into place, drifting further than fathomable.
Uninhabitable! Crawl back. Fix it, fix it now and fix it fast!

Zones of emptiness remove you from the throne, your right and honour.
A bother, tasks of supposed infinite simplicity amplified to mountains.
Knowledge trickles, fountains dry up as the reservoir is out of bounds.

The dream state marries reality, compounding the frazzled condition,
With remission, colours seep through with fragility; optical imagery creates scales of grey.
Lifelessness subdues the vibrancy that once existed; virility is dead!

The head makes sense of nonsense, when incensed and no incense calms.
Threat of harm, cerebrum defences engaged, strength of resolve tested.
Conflict against what resides where your chest is. Civil war.

Cognitively impaired, scared for fear of spiralling to a realm of no return,
Soon burning desires disappear when you learn you're unaware your surroundings.
Compounds in the space of the cerebellum chastise corporeality.

Reality metamorphosing into myth, the fight for survival must overcome.
No longer can you run, stand firm and battle for your freedom of thought.
Hold secure the lessons taught bring to the forefront of your perceptibility.

Me, myself and I.

71

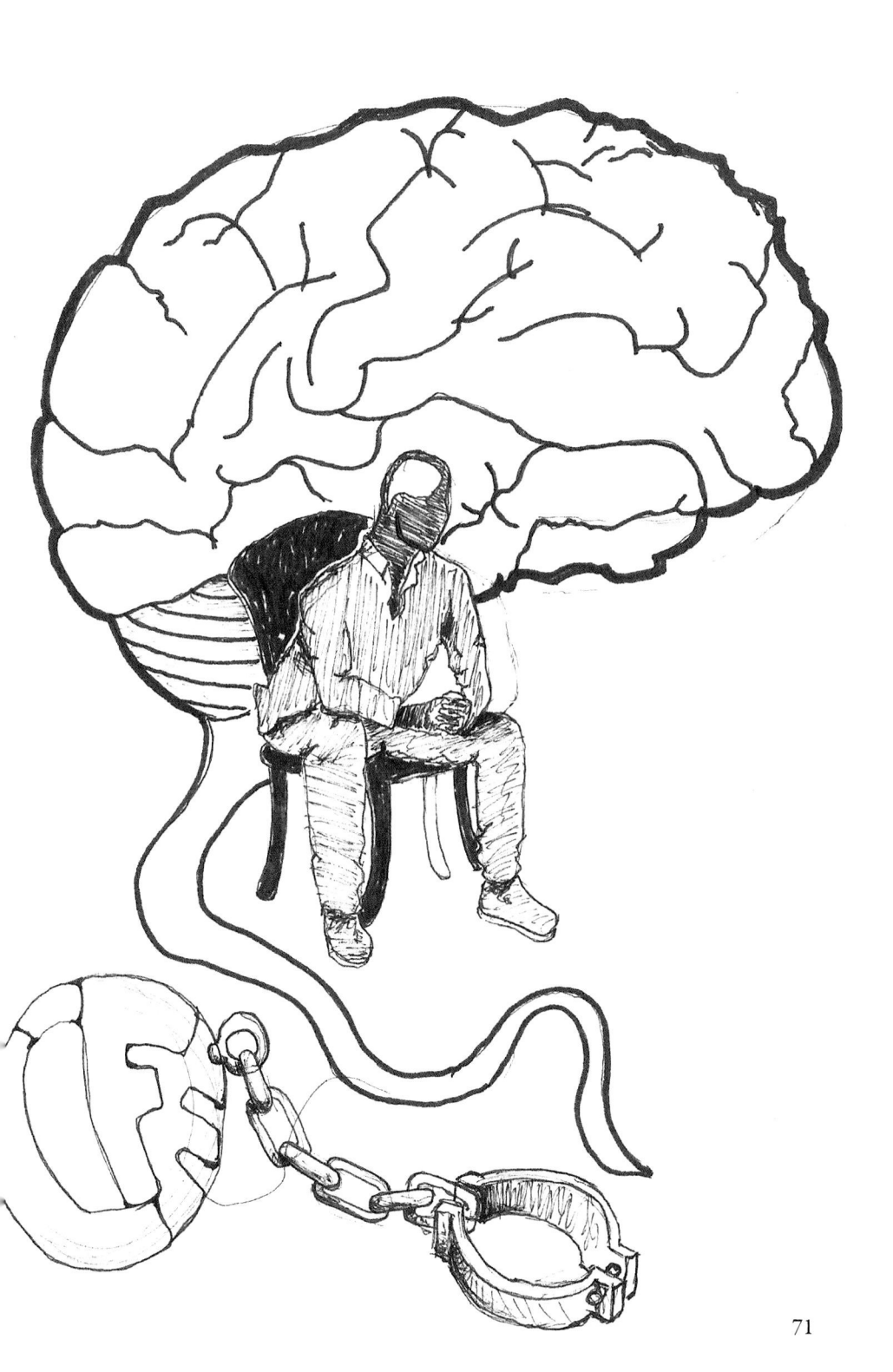

MOST OF MY TIME

It starts with a shower, a glance in the mirror.
Pondering the time about to be spent.

Why do I do this... every day? Is it the way I'm supposed to live?
Is this life or am I in another beings construct?
Answers remain unfounded, regardless of conversations occurring.

Occasional feeling - self-destruct. Push the button.
Ready! Finally... I think, I wonder.
Am I ready?
Or am I an automaton automatically operating on my set programme?

Waiting upon transport to collect this drone I call a body.
Bih, bih, bih, bih, bih, bih, bih, bih, bih, the sound logging this travelling entity.

8 hours on the clock, that's what I acknowledge.
Tick tock, tick tock, time motions smooth as a gravely road.
On closer inspection, an hour to arrive, an hour to depart.
The lies I've been told! Tis not an 8-hour day!
10 hours of work, eight to sleep and recuperate - six glorious to eat, socialise and repeat!

Staring at the computer screen, one zero zero one one zero one,
flashing faster than I can comprehend.
Binary living forms pictures of spreadsheets, words and imagery.
Computerised living for this organic brain it is enough to drive a
"man" insane.
Longing for interaction from another, long exhalations encourage
me to break concentration.

"Hello" and "how's your day?" Brings simple joy to this boy meets world.
12:30 - lunch, recharge for a further slog, would prefer a heart
pounding, mind jolting jog.
Difficult, but necessary, desk bound four more hours sweaty is not an
option as I feel the body begging for more.
The day drifts; riding the violent currents of boredom and
monotony, home time seems an eternity away.
Held captive as a prisoner of the 9-5, productivity cannot last more
than a few. The brain needs to live and the body follows.

Scream, protest and leap from the highest floor, crashing to my
demise. Obviously daydreaming; lids sealed over my eyes.
Further clarity why the windows remain shut; people
(if that's what I am) would escape through comfort of death, as reality smacks,
announcing, "You're stuck in a rut."
Cardiovascular activity continues, convincing me of my humanity,
as loud as it rhythmically pumps; I'm struggling to maintain my sanity.
4pm meeting, the conveyor belt transports us room bound,
we march robotically, in synchronisation taking our designated docking ports.

Silence deafens.

Monotonous tones reverberating from voice box to cochlea.
Computing ensues between the ears, mangled between reality and
dream state, escape route located at the rear.

Nodding commences in unison, signs of sleep or awareness, it is unknown.
Final task of the day, this congregation of consciousness,
mind mapping and brainstorming zone.

Relief as bags packed, monitors blacken and chairs swivel.
Long march to underground people muncher commences, ants, machine or man,
we are civil.

Reflections upon reflection, sweat mixes with scents akin to man.
One more hour to home, this state of forced roboticism must end,
finalise the escape plan.

Home; feeling human as food is consumed and freedom is felt.
Another day down, dreams of the weekend burn brightly at the forefront of my mind,
victory will be dealt.

A shower begins and ends each chapter. Wetness washes away the struggles,
mechanisms and circuits plugged in. Forever resist
the contracting captors.

Most of my time, provided at a set cost. Rights, privileges and liberties
never to be tossed.

A reminder I am human!

38438

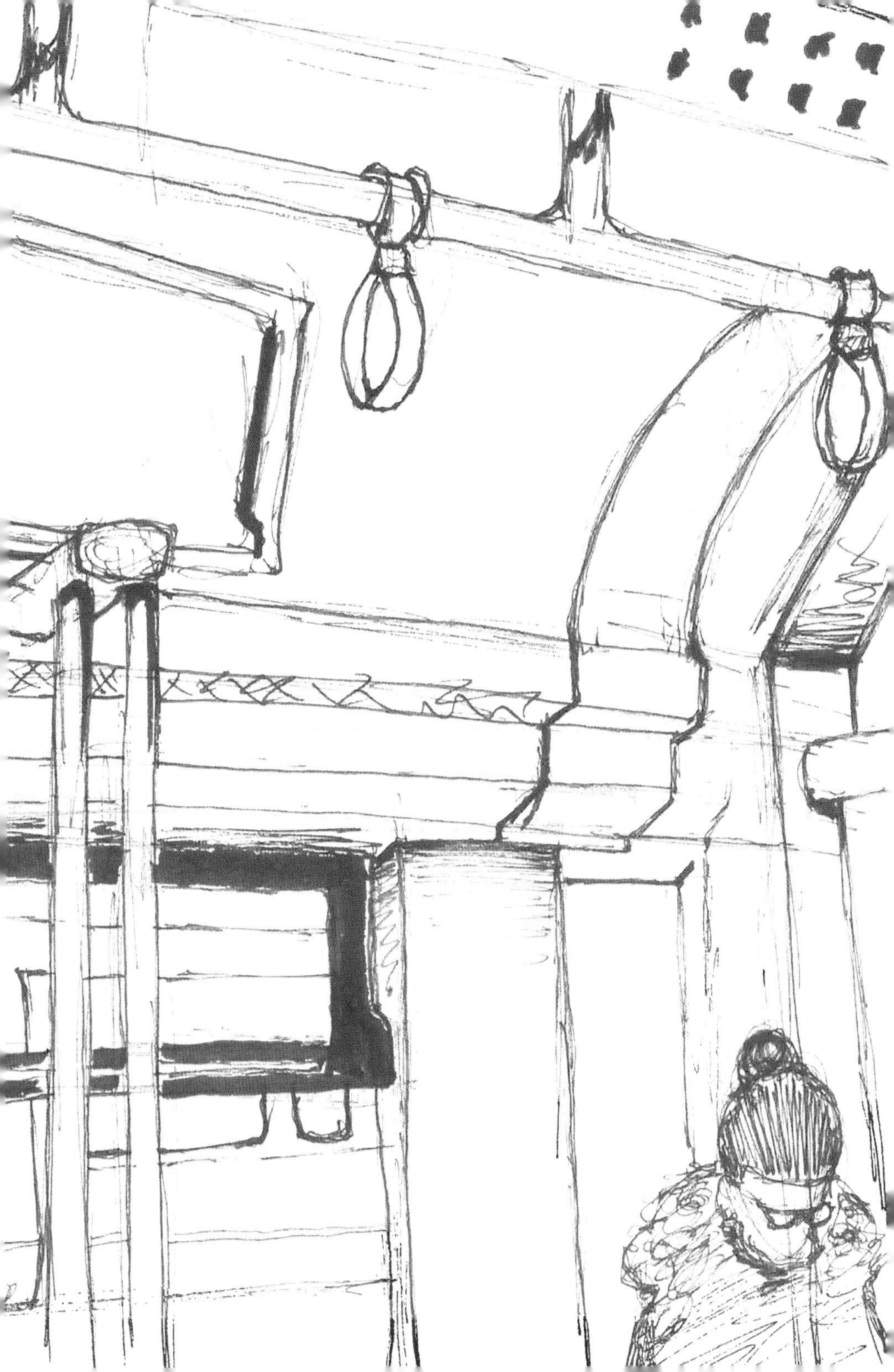

CONTROL

I totally lost it!

Cyah believe mi eyes. Da disrespect. Haffi bruk him up!
I totally lost it!
Yuh cyan tek man fi eediat. No way. Not today.
I totally lost it!
Raging red rivers flowin' through my every being,
I totally lost it!
People harangue me for peace. It's doing my damn nut
I totally lost it!
Voices rushing pass me eardrums, man's got nuttin' to say!
I totally lost it!
Noir, midnight and rouge are my dominating colours.
I totally lost it.
Ready to create my masterpiece, sadistic ideas will flourish!
I totally lost it.
Straight, up, down, across. My brushes begin to paint,
I totally lost it.
Heart is galloping, vision is narrowed. I'm fully focused.
I totally lost it...
Feeling invincible, faster than a speeding bullet, more powerful than a locomotive,
I totally lost it,
Nearly done painting. Splish, splash, drip, drop, and now a round of applause,
I totally lost it!

Breathing slowing, muscles throbbing, sweat pouring
I totally lost it;
Bones bruised, ego lifted and all is right with the world.
I totally lost it!
Vision clear, voices audible, my work here is certainly done
I totally lost it.
A mess was made, a man is ruined, I see the carnage
I totally lost it.
A woman is screaming a child is crying, there's overwhelming sadness
I totally lost it?
Lives are changed!
I totally lost it.
The pathway to this destination is unmemorable
I totally lost it?
Blue and red flash once again, descending upon me fast,
I totally lost it.
The idea of me is altered in an instant
I totally lost it,
Orders batter my ears, everything imperceptible but the loud pain in my arms.
I totally lost it.
The world starts spinning, up is down and concrete becomes intimate,
I totally lost it.
A visual melee of yellow, black and white
I totally lost it.

Finding myself sat back up, newfangled pains meander through my being,
I totally lost it.
Sequence of events, stumbling away from my present consciousness
I totally lost it?
Consequences now outweighing my pride, RAS!
I totally lost it.
Control?
I totally lost it!
Freedom?
I totally lost it!

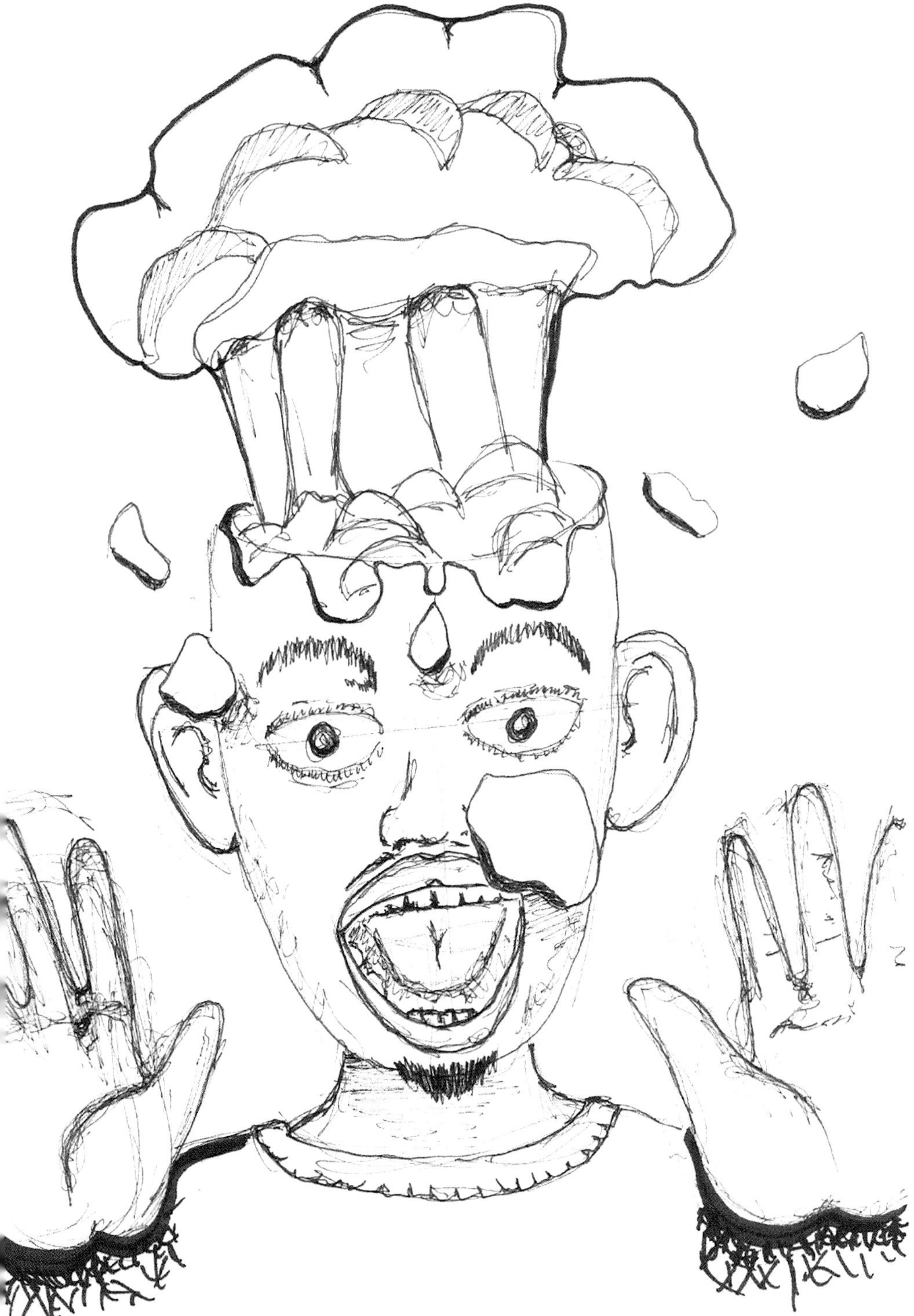

MUERTE

It is the all consuming, which nothing ever prepares us for.
An inescapable eventuality.
Millennia of lost souls, love, ideas and dreams never to return.
Swallowed up by grubs and worms.
Fortunes of the few live long past due, as the originators perish into nothingness.
Remembered if worthy.
Snatched at a moment's notice, no matter how lengthy and painful
the journey towards the spectacular finale.

The answer to all ails, problems, joys and pleasantries are the same,
with each version varying with this totality.
Transition from the plains of reality onwards, upwards, outwards.
Resistance is futile, freely fight and squirm.
Matters matter not as struggles are forgotten, dissipating permanently.
Leaving some distressed and nervy.
Tears, fears, stress and anguish linger as feelings escape one
to reside elsewhere, spiralling into the dark valley!

Kick ball, kick back, just kick it. Time spent as you choose, freedoms
enjoyed by many, then kick a bucket.
Acts of entitlement catches the unsuspecting as tomorrow isn't promised,
yet expectations speak otherwise,
Wrongdoings and good deeds tell a story of polar opposites,
with all conclusive results amounting to equality.
Vacation and staycation, locations aplenty, beaches and city breaks
are a prerequisite before the final destination.

Lovers of flowers, green fingers and botanists, display their
ultimate masterpiece by pushing up daisies.
Doctors' work is never done, with all actions working with futility, certain failure.
Win the battle, but never the war, unsurprised.
Minds ravaged and bodies abused through living precariously.
No rest for the wicked but all submit to permanent tranquillity.
Mortality is the commonality of all humanity.
Borders and languages cause divisions but all are united in ultimate expiration!

LETTING GO

The hardest part is the letting go.
Knowing your touch will fade out of existence.

People say, "Just let it go."
But there was a reason why I gripped so tight.

As does a mechanical vice.

It's time to let it all go.
Time however seems to crawl with your eternal absence.

Mimicking the drip of fresh paint.

Struggling to let go on a daily basis,
It's far easier to concede to the feelings of injustice.

Similar to a tree consumed by a hurricanes wind.

Why can't I let go?
Being forced to, it's something I just don't want to accept.

Like a dejected employee.

Can I let go?
There is no choice! My actions must, but the heart struggles.

Resembling the battle in tug of war.

Letting go could be easier.
This would mean that I couldn't have cared, right!

Much as a kid cares about a stone thrown.

I desperately want to let go.
The weight is unbearable, as I feel my spirit being crushed.

Comparable to a grape beneath an elephant's foot.

Letting go is the best thing!
Often those are the thoughts, but the feelings swirling around say there's something better.

Identical to choosing mince when you should have steak.

Let go of the good times.
The memories live long, strong and true.

Akin to powerfully mountainous regions of earth.

Someday I will let go.
Then the heart may become cold.

Lifeless as a canister of liquid nitrogen.

Once I have let go, expect no return back and observe the pain dissipate.

Fresh as a morning mist after the sunrise.

I have let go.
Now I can receive more.

Living as a half filled bottle, emptied and ready.

AU REVOIR

Like a sea breeze disappears upon the gentle rocking of the waves
I wave goodbye to days gone by of a younger me.
A younger me, anticipating what the world will be;
Cruel, harsh and unforgiving, just as a nighttime storm. Or snuggly and warm, though lying in a heated blanket? I think it will embrace however it unfolds. Living life is to be bold.
Unbeknownst to me 'IT' will be what I make it, with the power lurking beneath my skin, my time is wasted, collecting rubbish, bin!

Breathing fresh air into adolescent lungs, that delectable taste of youth, run. Feet interchange rapidly with no direction, all part of the fun. Happily tripping and cavorting in the endless folly of youth. Snappily changing, boundless choices winding and weaving as though tree roots. Speed is for the young, it'll never leave, finding pace overflows with limitless amounts, but we make the days count as haste surmounts the necessity for patience.
Playing with time and invincibility never to be lost.

There's always a cost, but no finance sits within the sewn receptacles of my pantaloons. Why would I need it when living breathing cash machines follow my every move? Sometimes I'm a spectacle. Things become smooth, as life is understood before it's overstood and I get into a groove. Where puberty kisses me tenderly, unlike the girls my body lusts for longingly. Biased to those sporting bosoms a plenty, now faced with rivalry of fellow chromosome Y. Losing the days I operated gently. Missing peaceful days gone by.

"Hi" words of a smelly guy. Fragrances of odours desired by few, nothing was said until it was said, who knew. Hygiene is a myth like a Minotaur marauding a maze. The armpits horrendous overtones leave you in a hazy daze. Knocking all senses a sunder from the figure they were assigned. Such a beauty to behold, check that delicious behind. Unlikely that my existence can be sold like a high priced item, reception is cold, but I still like 'em. Tough guy, soft guy, nice guys finish last. Loser!

Just like a teen movie I get cast, play a role or don't play at all. That's not my portion. I make the call. "Your exams are your life!" we are told at the end of school. Na! Don't be fooled. We mess, we joke and we live, no stress. It's time to give our brains a jolt, 5 years ramping those days are gone, feel the strain, bolt of lightening it's all superbly frightening. Unprepared! Scared is something I don't do successfully. Fail to prepare, prepare to fail. All hail the boffins doing it big, their game plan was sick. You can have it all; fame and fortune, take your pick.

Final hours, school gates no longer daunting. Corridors of tears, fights, chants and mischief I'll no more be haunting. Flaunting my ever best, puffed chest and male pride, the tide is with me. I see the sea awaiting me to be sailed with gusto. No choice, leave the year tens to reign, I must go. Excitement in my pants, you must know, I'm a big boy now. Time to bow out kid; all over, childhood you must rid. Paid the cost with my life, sixteen of my greatest years, mi ready! No fears! Sorrows tossed. Essential to lose the boy to become the man. Totally lost.

Love

Love is a thing that comes in many forms. However in a restrictive language such as English, we can be quite limited with our choice of descriptive words. We only have one word to describe all the varieties of love we experience as human beings.

The ancient Greeks had seven highly expressive and accurate words that encompassed the different forms of love. Personally, I feel we need these to be incorporated into the vocabulary of modern western society.

The seven types of love are as follows:
1. **Eros** - Sexual passion
2. **Philia** - Deep friendship
3. **Ludus** - Playful love
4. **Agape** - Neighborly love
5. **Storge** - Unconditional, familial love
6. **Pragma** - Longstanding love
7. **Philautia** - Love of the self

Something that I have said many times to my nearest and dearest is -
'A life without love is empty.'

This is something I truly believe. However the love is felt or experienced, without it a massive chasm of emptiness can be left. Making much of what we do feel pointless.

The effects of love and what they can inspire and encourage us to accomplish are tremendous. We read about many feats in mythology, newspapers and books of history. When you are fortunate enough to connect with someone who reciprocates your love, there is a power and purpose that you are filled with. This creates a potential to change your entire outlook on life.

Self love is an amazing thing. The love from within that is decribed by the Greeks as Philautia is one of the key foundations of our confidence, self-worth, building a sense of purpose and helping us fit in. Learning to love ourselves first, fully, helps us achieve a level of happiness that allows us to be 100% authentic and loving.
Even in the most testing of times and relationships.

Agape – This love seems to be severely lacking in many societies. The news around the world shows many atrocities being committed and I believe this is due to the absence of love beyond those we know personally. We all are connected and feed off the energies we emit.

More neighborly love will assist in the feeling of safety and protection that many of us need from our communities. Fear is a massive driving force for violence and other crimes.

Togetherness is born out of love.

Eros seems to be in abundance. In fact this seems to be what fuels societies every action. Schools, social media and traditional media appears to have overwhelming amounts of Eros based interaction being encouraged, while negating the other types that comprise all our relationships in some respect.

These poems stem from a host of personal experiences and observations made of friends and family closest to me. Some poems tell a weaving story that may have transpired over years, but is condensed into a few words to give a brief outook into the intensity of emotions that were felt at the time.

I have a love for the natural world, sensory and atmospheric experiences but most of these writings are about intimate relationships.

Some lovers have remained and others have passed with the hands of time.
Nevertheless all partook in sculpting the man that exists today.
Unknowing the future, there is more to come and things will manifest as they should, but never should love be absent.

Though there has been pain and anguish that has come hand in hand with love, there is certainly more blessings that are tied to this wonderfully complex emotion.

From the moment we are born, we are surrounded by it and develop our own versions. Ever growing and expanding, until the day we die someone will remind us of Love's underlying existence.

Feel it and allow love to permeate every aspect of your lives.

One Love!

(ODE TO) LOVE

You make us fall head over heels, injuries guaranteed
We slip and slide madly, deeply truly
Only fools rush in, complete consumption

Unsuspecting victims making declarations till time end
Intoxicating, many become sick, unable to stand or concentrate

Better experienced and lost, than total absence and,
A life without you is not worth living
Stuck in triangles with excessive and suffocating entanglements

You fill a life with elation and drive, ready to take on anything,
Instigating procreation, turning world's upside down
Eyes closed, open up to a new purpose of existence

Striking with a bullets force, the strong are weakened and,
The fragile are empowered as pure, concentrated essence fills them
Everlasting smiles, the curing of ails, boundless possibilities surround you

We speak of you conquering all, especially in the harshest times
All's fair with affairs of the heart or waging war
But those closest will mourn the untimely passing of souls bound by blood

Teenagers exist madly in it, with no view for much else
Absence grows fondness, but lack of presence pains

Economic status cannot acquire the truth, though many will try
Pain immeasurable courses through the veins, exploding hearts violently

Whilst magical moments take forever to mature, then last a lifetime
Growing old, firsts are unforgotten; memories don't tire

Energies transferred generationally,
That crazy thing called love

A-Z OF LOVE

Above all allegiances
Breast begets bold bravado, bringing boys begging because booty beckons. Babies born.
Creating cultural clashes, conversely culminating in coupled cohesion.
Delving deeply, devouring devotion diligently. Darkness disguises devilish dealings.
Everyone enjoys engrossed engagement, eventually entreating exhilarating erotic explosions.
Frolicking frivolously, forging friendships, forming families, from frequent fornication.
Getting girls, greeting guys, and graciously generating gratuitous gatherings.
Happily having humorous huddles.
Interacting intimately, initiating intense intercourse.
Jovially jabbering, just jesting. Justifiably.
Kinaesthetic kisses.
Love, lust, longing, licking, lingering looks. Lavish ladies live luxuriously,
luring lads without leniency.
Malevolence for mediocrity motivates man's movement. Maintaining modernity,
mischievous misdeeds make marriages.
Newlyweds need nothing, nurturing nostalgia.

Organising overdue opening of orifices, omnipotent operating
often overwhelm oneself orgasmically.
Practicing penetrative prowess proves powerful.
Passion is prominently presented.
Questioning quietness, Queens quarrel.
Respectful resolution requires remembrance of romance.
Reignite, rekindle and recharge recherché rendezvous.
Songs serenade seamlessly suggesting sexual stimulation.
Scintillating seduction, salacious surroundings. Someone's surely succumbing.
Touching, teasing, talking.
Terrific temptation triggers trouble.
Undulations unravel unspeakable understandings.
Voluptuous vixens, virile virtuosos valiantly vying for vaginal validation.
Winning without whining. Withdrawals wouldn't wash.
With wives wondering when waning will waken.
Xenia,
Yes, yes, yes, youth yearns.
Zealous zaftig, zestful and zany.

MY EMPRESS

My Empress!
Your flame! My fire!
You are my hearts desire.

Royalty!
No longer will I resist!
You are my crucial wish.

Supreme!
The significance you hold immeasurable.
Your scent! The epitome of pleasurable.

My Monarch!
All those clichés I evaded,
Present my entire love to you – I've been persuaded.

Ruler!
My heart is subjugated to your being.
Life is slaved to you and it's bizarrely freeing.

Queen!
Allow me to elevate us,
Our relationships foundations built on trust.

My Tsarina!
You are intellectually challenging and strengthening,
Support means all barriers I'm demolishing.

My Empress, you are royalty supreme,
My affections' monarch and ruler.
Queen! Tsarina! You are everything.
A blessing gifted from god...

You are *Woman*.

CONSCIENTIOUS

(**Read aloud** - Take a deep breath and exhale one time)

Conscientiousness of one and other can reduce stress particularly with your lover although happiness can be found under the covers it's not strictly the only relationship we deal with there is also friendship that can steal your heart so be thoughtful even when apart as consideration of a spouse or friend can bring humour and warmth to the house if you can't bend you will break be true to others and yourself never fake.

DAYZENITES

Starlight, existing in pure blackness. Look at that night sky!

'Twinkle twinkle little star, how I wonder what you are.'
Billions of hands extend to touch, you exist millions too far.

The utter allure and energetic magnificence, behold with the naked eye.

Bask beneath its evening glow,
nothing more glorious, pure romance with each astrological show.

Consumed by street lights and lanterns, often we narcissistically bypass their efforts.
Historically, viewpoint skyward to heavens, seeking answers for knowledge and comfort.

Pollution by luminance is misjudged and unnoticed, till it becomes a nuisance.

Stars they are, their heat emitted reaches cold, light from a bygone era we receive.

It's the times where candles reigned supreme, starlight star bright while we dream.
All stories contain unsung heroes of the infinite nightscape, potential for a mysterious theme.

Paint speckles across the galaxy, existence worthwhile.

Constellations, swirl as our world stands still, admire the brilliance with time to kill.

Innumerable take for granted beauty of sight,
forgoing simple complexities above as fancy takes flight.
Conspicuously, our resident bathe's us with loving heat. Blindness. Dangerous daylight.

Star crossed lovers entangled at night, exchange romantic gestures betwixt one and other.

Worlds apart, galaxies and star systems may hide life just like ours.

Beach walks in the summers eve, sand between the toes and no one wants to leave.
Songs play melodies sweet to the heart in the cover of darkness. Time to conceive.

We are given their shining gift, appreciate natures glory, as we relax in starlight glow.

City dwellers and country folk, luxury suburbanites and beach goers gaze above; destinies built on wishes emanating from love.

EYE YELL

I'm hot, hot and flustered.

That sweet elixir, decadent and effervescent.
The tongue jumps with elation as you trickle down,
Consumption is the overwhelming desire, fighting is futile.
Delicious! I already know, we understand each other.
You slip, slide and soothe as you splash awaiting surfaces,
Guzzle and gulp! I am insatiable. Keep it coming ever more.

I'm overcome and a shiver attacks my calcium structure.
Nonsense is the word; magnificent conjuring's of your essence,
Bathe me in your stickiness I want to suffocate and drown.
All pathways are closed, as surroundings become thick and cramped.
Nothing else in this moment surpasses your deathly glory.
I am consumed with love, yearning and infatuation like no other.

Everything in my body screams you're wrong for me,
Brain freezes, superseding all logic, violently and swiftly. I must act.
Quivers travel spinally, a true delight between my fingers, squeeze I must.
So precious and fragile is your body, destruction is inevitable!
Relationship is doomed, destiny promises; impossible to navigate otherwise.
We must succumb to temptation and indulge in pure pleasure.

You crumble in my hands, the pressure overwhelms you, I can see.
Your juices run rampant, oozing from every orifice and crack.
I've had my fill of you, but cannot stop; gorged on your sweetness,
Indulgence consumes me; I gaze upon you, suddenly filled with nausea.
The sight of you becomes one of distaste, how things switch so expeditiously.
Deep down in my heart, feelings remain; this negativity is temporary.

I love you more than a man should; my actions speak loudly, possibly?
I hold you tight, never relenting; I need you in my life!
You've always been there in my time of need, cooling me whenever heated.
My hands are sticky, my mouth is wet and eyes turn to exit the situation.
I must cleanse myself of this experience, returning home filthy is no option.
My woman awaits, ready to satisfy me, but my hunger has been sated.

You irresistible and naughty temptation... Eyes scream for Ice Cream.

KING FOR A QUEEN

Bow to you, I submit.
Fight for you, never quit.
Live for you, always, forever.
Both of us remain together.

Smile, laugh, tease and cry,
Satisfied, nothing I won't try.
Enjoying each of our days,
Thankful and grateful, giving praise.

Beauty, intelligence, faithfulness and true,
Nothing else needed but you.
The air that you breath,
I could have never conceived,

The path that you walk,
Constant pleasure hearing you talk.
To give you my offspring,
My love prevails over everything.

Combined our future is bright,
Our excitements at maximum height.
For you, I'm always available,
For all others, I'm unattainable.

Thinking of you constantly, always.
Because of you, better days.
Honour and protection you deserve,
Our love I'll always preserve.

Believe in and trust me,
Depend on your king thoroughly.
Your warm and voluptuous figure
reminds me I'm a winner.

Elevate you above all others,
With romance you'll be smothered.
I will cherish and adore,
You'll not want for more.

Strolls in gardens and parks,
Whispering sweet nothings after dark.
You are my life's Queen,
My Kingdom you'll reign supreme.

Graciously make me your King.
Without hesitation, accept this ring.

A King for a Queen.

EQUILATERAL

You want me!
I want her!
She wants him!
Who wins?

We try, but my mind is on her.
She chases, but never catches him.
You work hard and it doesn't pay off.
Who wins?

Time stands still for you.
Everything moves slowly for me.
Life moves too fast for her.
Who wins?

You're tired!
I'm tired!
She's tired!
Who wins?

You move on,
I make a change,
She instigates a difference,
We may win!

Life goes on.

Winning.

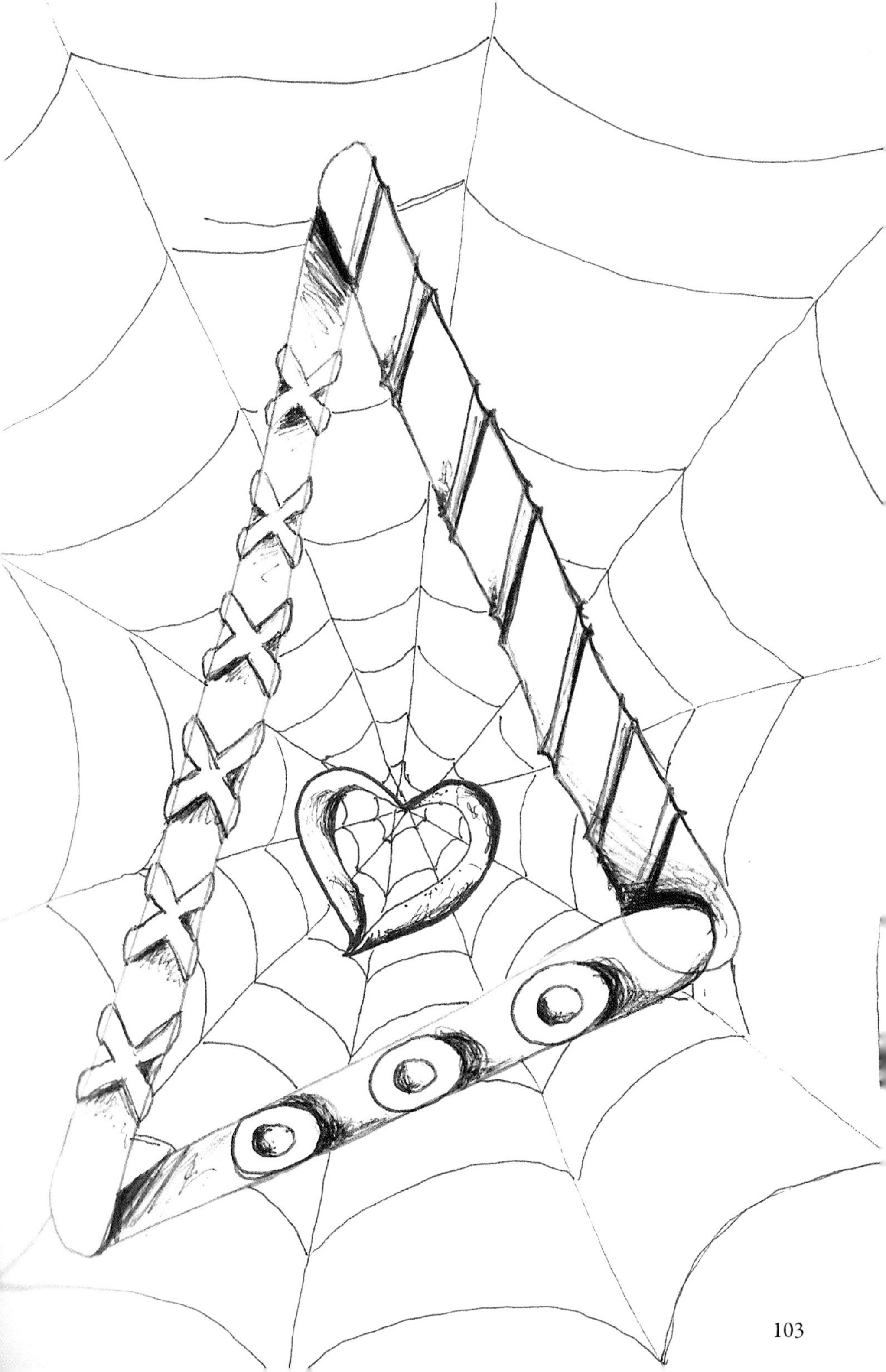

BEAST

There's that crazy infatuation.
To tame and control that which is born to roam.
Well that's the result if I show you the beauty, however...
I only ever show the beast!

That is the beauty of the nature,
which is the nature of the beast,
nature is wild, I'm wild by nature!
"Too wild sometimes" she would say.

Not everything wild must be violent and dangerous.
Untamed, hard to manage, exciting and thrilling.
These are the things you should seek.
Wild is free and unbridled. It is adventure, it is a spirit born with no bounds.

Why do we try to tame the savage beast?
This is not how you found it, yet you want a transformation.
The transformation you instigate robs all the characteristics and
traits that entice you.

Apex predator, beasts in their territory, masters over prey
and protectors of the weak.
Prey can be weak or strong. The stronger the adversary,
the better the challenge. That challenge betters the beast.

A beast lives by instinct, but a man thrives by his own derived code.
Life determines the prominence of these natural characteristics.
In this world, the man and the beast are one and the same.
One will please and fulfil, the other is sure to consume.

Man or Beast to which is your circumstance better suited?

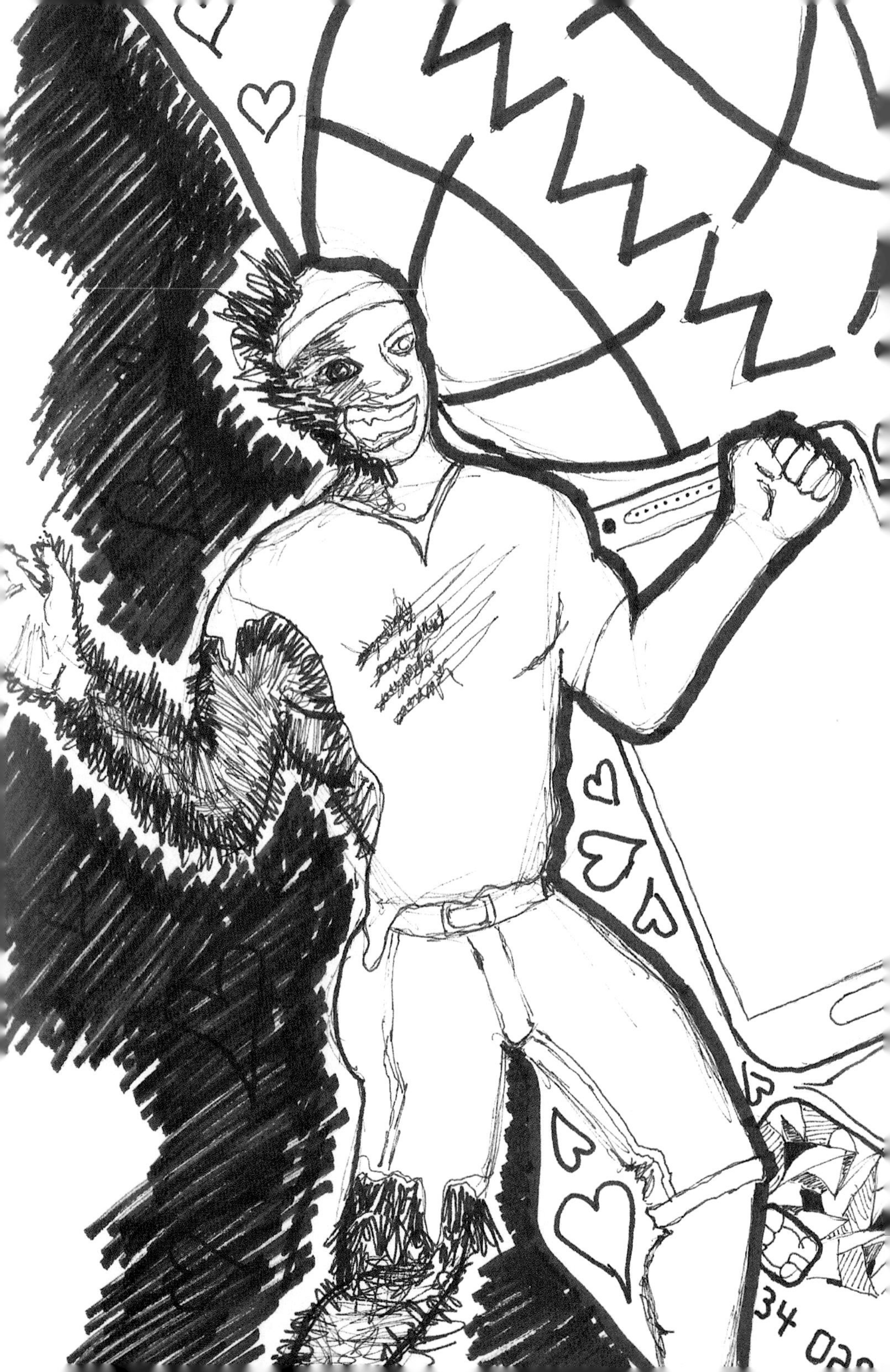
34 02

TOGETHER. FOREVER. NEVER

Decisions!

You say we should go right, so that's where we travel.
A road you've decided you want us to explore, I was a willing companion.
We try something new, embrace the challenge, have fun, that's life.
Moments later as the wind changes, it all seems to unravel.
I was strong, I was true, I thought I'd be your everything: your champion.
The signs were screaming, turn back, troubles are definitely coming; it's going to be rife.

Those warnings bypassed me. I was deaf. I was blind. Only you I could see or hear.
You appeared focused, but you were shaking, obviously, you were frightened.
The whispers grew louder, you heard more and me, I heard less.
None of that mattered; I was your protector there was nothing for you to fear.
Clearly, there was no belief as you started to sweat and your anxiety heightened.
This was my time to hold and reassure you. I felt your closeness,
but I could not feel the steady heartbeat in your chest.

Feeling cold and shivering, I attempted to warm you up. Wrapped my coat around you,
took you into my arms.
This time I wasn't enough, you moved away, you began to retreat.
You're walking backwards, slowly, with purpose; my senses are no longer obstructed.
What's going on? If you keep drifting away, you'll end up being vulnerable to harm.
Come back. Where are you going? We should continue to press forward! Shift your feet!
I've started to beat down the trail, making it suitable for us; a clear walkway is being constructed.

Evidently, it's too late. Your mind is made up; you're determined to flee. With that distance, I am powerless to safeguard you.

Worry has commenced overcoming my internal calm; nevertheless, I refuse to display my weakness. I must maintain composure.

The trouble or danger isn't apparent to me, so I am swept with confusion; the decision to embark on this journey was based on your spirits desire.

My eyes gaze upon you, the departing pace quickens, watching you disappear hastily in the opposite direction, I wonder what to do.

Scream and shout, I know no better. You're running to the place you suspect you need to be, disregarding your exposure.

Heading back towards the known, the unsurprising and the simple, I no longer need this in my hand, this torch, this fire.

Time for me to make a return journey, slower, with less vigor. I have no yearning to trek this road alone.

We are now together travelling in the same direction once more, however we are clearly separate.

Catching you is impossible, there's no looking over your shoulder, no more are you concerned for our wellbeing.

It's painful witnessing your departure, my strength remains, I will survive any situation that may occur now I know I'm on my own.

Feeling trepidation, I bid you farewell, reach safe. Abandoned, now it's about myself, you I must alienate.

All is different; my world has permanently changed, for you I was becoming a better man, now my behaviour may become obscene.

The choices we make shape our future. Our past, whether unpleasant or picturesque contours our decisions.
Our present is constructed through the collaboration or our dreams and reality.
Live. Laugh. Love. Be true to yourself and walk your own path to be happy.
As I continue on this road, I can see much more for myself, I must strive for greatness and follow this vision.
I have consigned myself to accepting the truth; there really is no you and me.
Cos boy. Now. I'm doing my own ting. I'll catch you on the other side, baby.

FUN AND GAMES

We are the playas
We are the ones you want but can never have.
We are the ones that make your heart quiver and your ladylove sing.
We are the playas
We are the ones that you meet at work, that help your day go by.
We are the ones who never stop until the panties drop.
We are the playas.
We are the ones that your mum would love and your dad is sure to hate.
We are the ones who will do everything, but make you work hard for a date
We are the playas
We are the ones who make you laugh and can make you cry.
We are the ones who you desire to see but are hard to find,
We are the playas
We are the ones who you can call for anytime but available some of the time.
We are the ones who, will call on you in our time of need with passion in the voice,
We are the playas
We are the ones that hug and kiss and squeeze you.
We are the ones that don't make promises to never leave you.
We are the playas
We are the ones that stand the test of time, returning like a boomerang.

We are the ones that will bring you more pleasurable moments
than the rest!
We are the playas
We are the ones that your people warned you about.
We are the ones that scream out 'danger!'
We are the playas
We are the ones that bring a thrill and a twist,
We are the ones that keep you on your toes, full of surprises.
We are the playas.
We are the ones
We are the ones that bring
The pleasure
The fun
The laughter
The jokes
The danger
The joy
The suspense
The thrill
The desire
The passion
The lust
The play
We bring you to the game
We are the playas!

TWILIGHT CAVORTING

We dance under di moonlit sky...

Her skin shimmered wid wonderful hues of brown 'n' gold.

Liming was di requirement an liming was di choice.

Nothing else to do but join di masses, stars speckle darkness, perfect timing, everything jump up, whine up yuh waist: be bold!

Rum flows, harsh an fiery, nothing else tastes sweeter. But, sounds of her voice...

Captivated, figures locked by our eyes.

Exquisite features, her face hypnotizes.
Hands caress a body carved from pure ebony, she's expensive.

Her lips quiver an body shudders, feeling di strength of my embrace.
Supple body moves wid di riddim of a seductress.

Music pierces, gluing entwined souls, drowning out other vixens an braddas.

Perfume an perspiration mix, an intoxicating scent of tropical love.
She glistens, wildly irresistible temptress.

Passions fire rages, subtlety dies!

Lips painted rouge part to whisper buttery unheard words. Ears tingle; delightful.

Synchronised riddim slows, bosom compressed gently against chest.

Bodily heat melts di room, liquor fuels di flames. We fight to stay civilised.
Our struggle is real, loose clothing stifles.

Drums muffle heart beats. Thirst for her, she covets me. Seductions unrest.

Our dances language of love ostentatiously tells no lies.

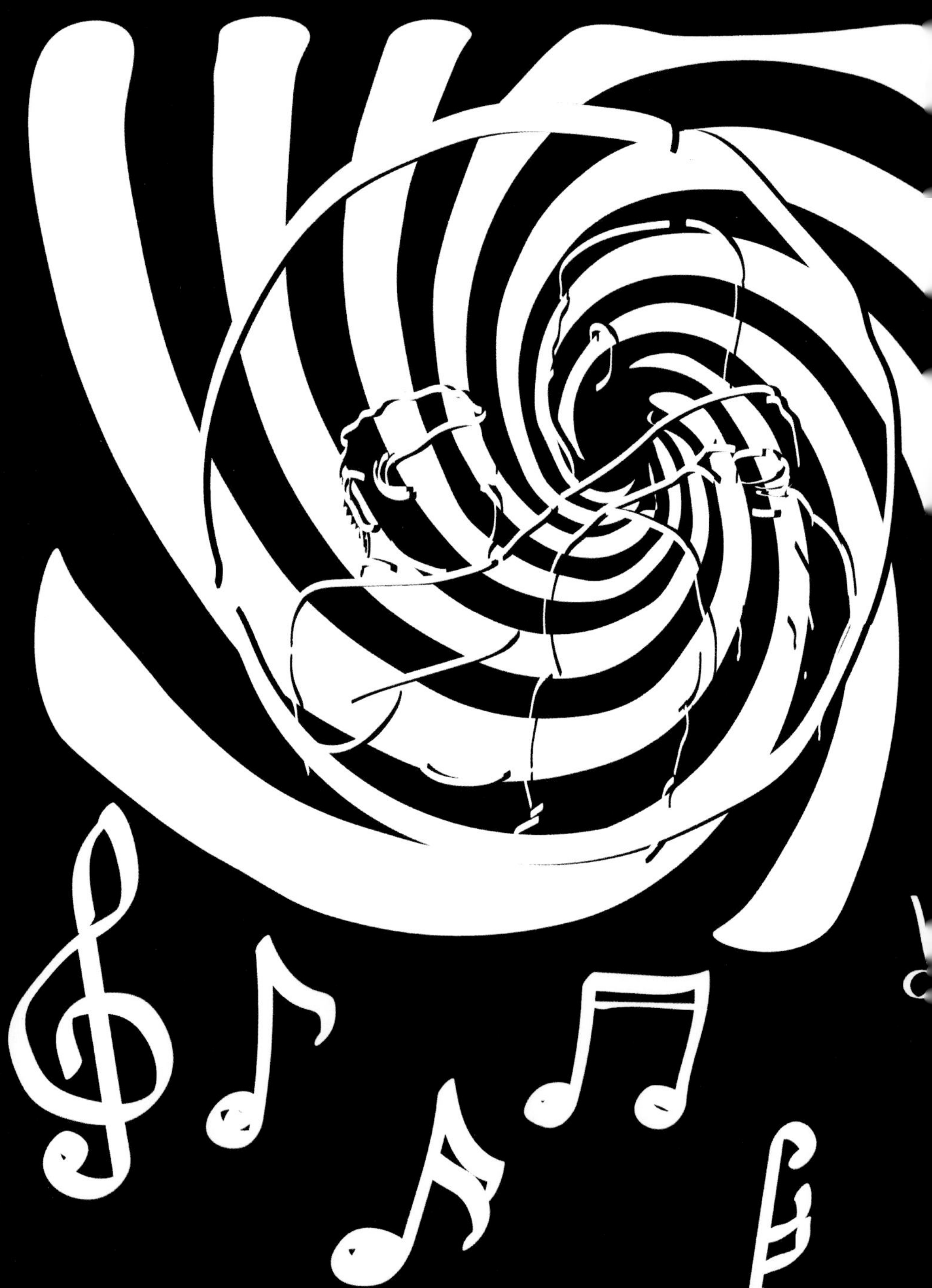

CIRCULINITY

Such is the repayment bestowed upon her.
He casts his final doorway shadow,
He turns and bares his teeth, fiercely!

Mercilessly and ruthlessly, he preyed!
Callously and purposefully he lied.
There was no compassion, evidently.
Eventually it will all unravel, messily.
Leaving hearts, and minds temporarily,
Unable to love or fathom reality.

Subsequently worlds were left tattily,
Hungrily awaiting satisfactory resolve.
No resolution was to be found, unfortunately.
Passionately he kissed the next, dishonourably.
Motive's clear, only to one, obviously.
His life was being lead erotically.

Graciously and humbly, he accepted gifts.
Physically and mentally, all was offered.
Everything embraced? No! Only bodily.
Emotionally, he rejected them, aggressively.
Vacant and absent, the void grew enormously,
Requirement for more was fed insatiably.

Gallantly, lovers were adorned sensibly,
Specifically targeting questioning souls.
No respite was to be given, tenaciously.
Sensuously he undressed the Miss, elegantly,
Body heaving, intentions overwhelm her, thoroughly.
His mind drifts to other pleasantries, whimsically.

Viciously and decisively, he hunted.
Ignorantly and innocently they fell.
Remorse had no existence, just ferocity!
Subconsciously, a longing for love internally,
These foreign feelings, ignored fruitlessly.
Meaningless actions growing fervently,

Destructively, between loves he wondered aimlessly,
Questioningly observing life's construct.
Situation-ships' black holes consume him, almost justly,
Rightly, he deserves reprisals, perhaps violently?
Observations foretells a life of diminished longevity,
His Immersive relationships speak of impending fatality.

Menacingly and unrecognisably he transformed,
Ugly and grotesque! Naked eye beauty.
Socially, murdered every way, assaulted spiritually,
Empty vessel, riddled with apertures sporadically,
Scarce substances required for repair urgently!
Peril loiters horizontally, vertically, diagonally.

Sharply victim spotted. Capture! Kill easily!
Diabolically old habits resurface, tranquil reversal,
Routine resumes, progression with simplicity.
Interestingly, minutiae of differences unnoticed, distinctly.
Unaware of the time passing, the victim lives exuberantly,
His prey becomes plaything, turns to keep sake, subtly.

Unwittingly and ignorantly Intertwined, his life's shared,
Irrationally and fervidly reignited, life brings purpose.
Daily, senses and sensibility evaporate like yesterday.
She provided respite from a term of savagery,
Consumed by desire and compassion, weakness ensues vividly.
His lover adorns him with preciousness constantly.

Aptly behaving as a feeder, gluttony vanished permanently.
Incomprehensibly masses of matter fill the void.
Revealed emotionally, exposing all his vulnerability.
Totally available for this person, this woman. Amazingly.
Protection, his physical, stability, his mental – unconditionally.
Humbly he gifts his being to her uncompromisingly.

Exceedingly and indisputably more to this situation than eroticism.
Discernibly and loyally, his motives clear and transparent.
Faithfully, with honour and passion he kissed deeply.
The resolution was discovered, finally!
A resolve to match his angst, hunger sated assuredly.
His tattered world reconfigured peaceably.

Proudly unable to love or fathom reality.
Heartlessly mindless. Cold permanently.
Undoubtedly, it all unravels, messily.
Sweetly there was no compassion, evidently.
Callously and purposefully she lied – Zealously.
Mercilessly and ruthlessly she preyed. Harmoniously.

She turns and bares her teeth, fiercely!
She casts her final doorway shadow.
Such is the repayment bestowed upon him!

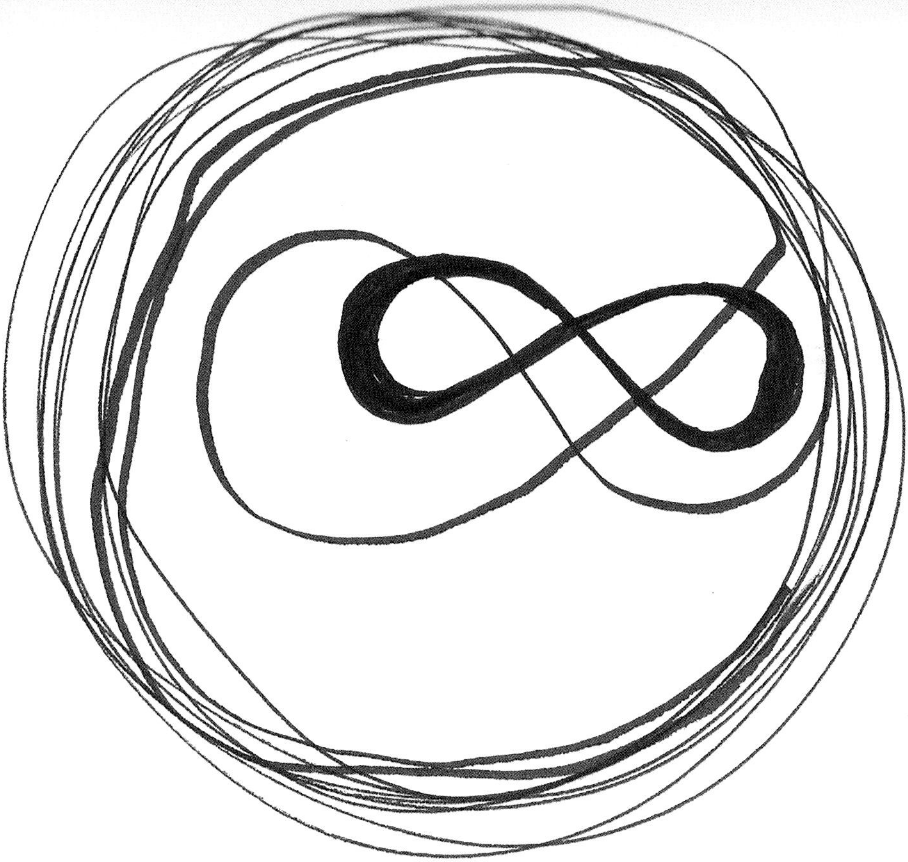

ADIEU

That touch, that everlasting embrace that beckons you in the night,
unforgettable is the first time and nothing will ever be the same,
smelling you brought an aroma of success and dreams made true,

future plans, laughter, frolics and hijinks we indulged happily,
it's frequently impossible to comprehend the final caress: what a fright,
memories of the conclusion, utterly painful as you didn't remain,

fragrances conjure feelings of failure; a nightmare living true,
the end could be crushing when accepting the reality,
it's hard to believe, but it really didn't last forever. I bid you adieu.